POLICE AUTHORITY
AND THE RIGHTS OF THE INDIVIDUAL

Police Authority and the Rights of the Individual

Sidney H. Asch

ARC BOOKS
New York

An ARC BOOK,
published by ARCO PUBLISHING COMPANY, Inc.
219 Park Avenue South, New York, N.Y. 10003

First ARC Printing, 1971

Library of Congress Catalog Card Number 97-146117

ISBN 0-668-02426-7

Printed in the United States of America

Contents

Introduction to the Revised Edition

Police Authority and the Rights of the Individual serves a valuable purpose. It brings to the lay reader a clear and concise explanation of some of the implications that have stemmed from the decisions of the United States Supreme Court in *Miranda* v. *Arizona* and related cases. The report of the President's Commission on Law Enforcement and the Administration of Justice, *The Challenge of Crime in a Free Society,* is woven through the text of the edition with skill and impact.

It is quite clear that Judge Asch had a limited but important objective in writing this book: to set forth in uncomplicated fashion police procedures as they relate to the criminal suspect. He has accomplished his goal, giving the reader a clear picture of the law relating to arrest, detention, search and seizure, confessions, right to counsel, and bail. While certainly not a technical legal treatise (and not intended as such), it is useful as a layman's handbook, written in an unpretentious style and employing actual cases to illustrate the various procedures.

Judge Asch has assumed a stance of objectivity, presenting materials that reflect divergent opinions concerning the validity of police procedures. On the first page of the book, he says: "It has been a slow and tortuous process since 1215 A.D. when the *Magna Charta* was signed by King John at Runnymede, which began the slow march of the law to evolve the procedures and institutions that protect the accused from the police apparatus of the state." With these words he implies that the recent Supreme Court decisions were not only necessary but long overdue. On the other hand, Judge Asch agrees with many critics of the Court decisions, declaring: "The job of the policeman is . . . not a . . . happy one. Recent judicial decisions relating to arrests, confessions, search and seizure, and the right to a lawyer, have made police efforts more difficult."

But difficulty in enforcement is not the sole criterion of criminal justice. A democratic society must and does not reject expediency as an end in itself. As police officers assume new roles in the structure of American society, their work may be eased somewhat by more understanding on the part of the community of who they are, what they do, and the limits of their authority.

Judge Asch's book is a first-rate source for this information. Its theme can be found in his succinct statement: "The central issue of our time appears to be the increasing conflict between the assertion of authority and the maintenance of individual freedom."

One of the obvious conclusions to be drawn from the author's work is that an urgent need exists for higher standards of selection, training, and education of police and other criminal justice personnel. The more sophisticated needs and demands of the community, the growing complexity of urban life, and the dawn of a new era of social control require the further professionalization of the police officer. This can and will be accomplished by better pay and working conditions (an expression of community regard), more extensive training, and the exposure of police and potential recruits to a liberal arts education.

As part of this thrust towards professionalization, it is necessary that we, every one of us, learn and understand the police structure, police procedures, and the place of police in American society. For basic information, presented clearly in outline form, *Police Authority and the Rights of the Individual* is excellent.

LEONARD E. REISMAN
President, John Jay College of
Criminal Justice

POLICE AUTHORITY
AND THE RIGHTS OF THE INDIVIDUAL

I.
The Policeman and Preliminary Criminal Procedures

THE CENTRAL ISSUE of our time appears to be the increasing conflict between the assertion of authority and the maintenance of individual freedom. Dr. Sigmund Freud posed this problem in psychoanalytic terms as one of the major "discontents" of civilization. Whether we consider the problem from the point of view of the relationship of the economic system to the small businessman, or whether we consider it from the aspect of the centralization of governmental power as against the retention of such power in the hands of local units of government or of the people, we have a reflection of the same conflict. The most critical area of confrontation is that which occurs between the policeman and the citizen.

What is sometimes forgotten is that community standards of protection for John Doe are steadily rising. It is quite easy to overlook the centuries during which the thumbscrew, the wheel, the rack, trial by fire, Chinese water torture, and other simple but effective police methods were commonly employed. Equally drastic techniques and tools were used in the past in detaining and arresting people who were *persona non grata* to those in power, in what passed for fair trials, to secure confessions. The terminal stages in criminal justice were equally direct, effective, and without regard to technical niceties. The felon was given hemlock, drawn and quartered, boiled in oil, burned at the stake, tossed to the lions, or accorded comparable treatment.

Certainly part of the reason we are so concerned with the rights of individuals today is that we have come to expect that these rights will be respected. It has been a slow and tortuous process since 1215 A.D. when the *Magna Charta* was signed by King John at Runnymede, which began the slow march of the law to evolve the procedures and institutions that protect the accused from the police apparatus of the state.

This issue—including both the police position and the position of

1

those who urge restrictions on the police—is one that is important to each one of us in terms of direct impact. It is entirely possible that any citizen may be arrested and kept in jail overnight because of a traffic-law violation. A person falling asleep on the subway may be held as a vagrant. An argument in the street may be construed as disorderly conduct with resulting arrest and detention. And it is important that the citizen be concerned about charges of police brutality, forced confessions, failure to be represented by a lawyer, and violation of the rights of minority groups.

The Policeman's Lot

The job of the policeman is often not a very happy one. Recent judicial decisions relating to arrests, confessions, search and seizure, and the right to a lawyer, have made police efforts more difficult. First, it is difficult for a policeman (it is even difficult for a lawyer) to understand and apply the rules of the United States Supreme Court, and other courts, in this field. Second, the police and prosecutors, almost to a man, feel that these legal restrictions often permit criminals to go scot free and thus encourage crime.

Charles S. Desmond, Chief Judge of the New York Court of Appeals, recently declared, with respect to the new approach by the Supreme Court, that "[it has] the everyday practical effect . . . of depriving the public, not just the prosecutors and the police, of reliable, convincing, real evidence. What this approach does is insure and safeguard the professional criminal, especially the narcotics dealer and gambler," asserted Judge Desmond. It does not protect the ordinary citizen, "who never needs it."

Consider the following examples:

Toward midnight one night, a conscientious policeman, making his rounds, noticed a man pulling a large, unwieldy valise along the sidewalk. Tired from his efforts, the man paused at a public bench, dragged the suitcase behind it, and sat down to rest. The police officer went up to the man and asked him about the valise. The man on the bench seemed surprised and asked, "What valise?" When the man persisted in refusing to answer the policeman's queries, he was taken to the station house. There it was ascertained that the valise contained the haul of a burglary. The policeman had relied simply on his powers of observation and had followed a hunch based on long experience. However, since he had not known of the commission of the burglary at the time when he went up to the defendant, interrogated him, and detained him, the court ruled that it was not proper to seize the evidence of the burglary, and the arrest was deemed unlawful. The case against the defendant was dismissed.[1]

In another instance, a police captain, while making his tour of duty at about four-thirty one afternoon, noticed a young man carrying what appeared to be an expensive piece of luggage. The police officer, feeling that something was wrong, asked him a few questions. By way of explanation, the young man stated that the luggage belonged to a friend, whom he described only in vague terms.

The captain then directed the young man to get into the police car along with the luggage, and the police undertook to find the "friend." It soon became clear that the friend did not exist. The young man was driven to the office of the detective squad. There he confessed that he had stolen the valise from an automobile he had broken into. The court, however, refused to consider the proceeds and evidence of the crime on the grounds that the temporary detention of the defendant constituted an unlawful arrest.[2]

A few years ago, shortly after New Year's Eve, an alert policeman saw an automobile with its engine running and its trunk lid ajar parked in front of a Western Union office. Although he was still some distance away, he noticed two men straining to lift a heavy object into the trunk of the car. As they pulled away, the officer summoned a passing automobile and, after a chase, stopped the car and held the two men. After checking, he learned that the Western Union office had been broken into. The two men and their automobile were taken to the police station. The car trunk was found to contain a safe with the name "Western Union" painted on it, as well as a fine assortment of burglar tools. The case against the defendants was dismissed on the theory that their initial arrest, predicated "on mere suspicion sparked by a keen intuition," was illegal.[3]

From the point of view of the policeman on the beat, such rulings place an intolerable burden of decision on him, shackling him in the performance of his duty.

Law Enforcement and Enforcement of Citizens' Rights

Crime in the streets projects a terrifying picture in twentieth-century America. The President of the United States, in his message to Congress of March 8, 1965, stated: "Crime is in America's midst. Since 1940 the crime rate in this country has doubled. It has increased five times as fast as our population since 1958."

It may well be that this widespread fear is disproportionate to the realistic situation. It is possible that an analysis in depth of the statistics on crime would show a more encouraging—or at least a less discouraging—picture. Futhermore, it is certain that the vast panoply of officialdom, the judges, the legislators, the prosecutors, the police, all those engaged in the business of law and order, are not going soft on crime.

Why then is there heard the hue and cry for stricter enforcement of the law? It has been urged that the threat of an overwhelming crime wave is not a sufficient explanation. One suspects that the emphasis on law enforcement may be occasioned by a sense of guilt with respect to evasion of legal structures. And we are also becoming increasingly insecure in a world in which conventions, moral codes, and rules of law no longer seem to apply as they did in those halcyon days of peace and serenity enjoyed by our fathers (or did they ever exist?). It is interesting to note that, psychologically, the call for stricter law enforcement seems to spring from the same sources as do the attacks on civil liberties that are heard from time to time. What is obviously required is more study of this phenomenon by social historians, psychologists and sociologists, as well as by lawyers.

Gunnar Myrdal, the Nobel Prize winner, points out in his *The American Dilemma* that there have always been two ambivalent currents in American life. On the one hand, there has been an emphasis on enactment of more and more laws. On the other, there has been an impatience with the restraints imposed by the strictures of the law. There has often been a willingness to resort to violent action, to a forceful rejection of the more plodding, more devious processes of the law. This dichotomy in approach continues to plague law-enforcement officials. Judge Learned Hand, speaking of a roundup of vagrants and petty criminals by Grover Whalen, when he was New York City police commissioner, amid the general approval of such actions by the community leaders, pointed out that these worthy citizens would bridle at the thought that someone should be punished at official whim without evidence of guilt. Said Judge Hand: "They are loyal to our institutions in the abstract, but they do not mean to take them too seriously in application."

And more recently another New York City police commissioner, Michael J. Murphy, complained that what the Supreme Court is doing "is akin to requiring one boxer to fight by the Marquis of Queensberry rules while permitting the other to butt, gouge, and bite."

One cannot help but be sympathetic with the commissioner's objective. Yet the implications raise serious questions. Is he saying he would like the police not to have to obey the law in the process of enforcing it? The police, he believes, should have the right to use the same criminal methods—"to butt, gouge, and bite"—as the criminals from whom they seek to protect society. It does not take great reflection to understand that by permitting the police to use criminal tactics we do not decrease the problem of crime in America, we increase it. No segment of the population, not the law enforcers, not even the Chief of Police, can be permitted to flout the law.

If the history of the twentieth century has taught us anything, it should have hammered home the lesson that one does not create a more law-abiding community by encouraging those in authority to feel that they are above the law. A distinguishing characteristic of a civilized community is its ability to bear the frustrations of a complex society in a rational way without giving in to the temptation to strike back blindly outside the law. The threat from the lawless, those who threaten the security of our streets and the safety of our homes, is not diminished by encouraging the law officer to become lawless.

The counterpoint of majority rule and minority right is the essential element in the symphony of our democracy. Still another former police commissioner, Vincent L. Broderick, apparently understands this aspect of the American system. At the time he was sworn in, he said: "I pledge that while I am Police Commissioner, the Police Department will strive toward . . . the ultimate end that every law-abiding citizen . . . and this includes every member of every minority group, and every policeman as well . . ., may be free to enjoy the liberty which such a climate will make possible."[4]

Judge Irving R. Kaufman, of the United States Court of Appeals, Second Circuit, has stated the pragmatic nature of the balance between majority rule and minority rights, in the context of the conflict between individual rights and the maintenance of public security. "Do we follow the lesson of history, which, according to Mr. Justice Brennan, proves that tolerance of short-cut methods in law enforcement impairs its enduring effectiveness? Or, on the other hand, do we heed Chief Judge Lumbard's warning that before we impose additional restrictions on the police we should display great caution, lest in the desire to protect individual rights the larger and greater right of all the people to be secure in their persons and in their homes becomes secondary? It is risky to give absolute and final answers, for just as police work cannot be equated to totalitarian oppression, so devotion to constitutional principles is not equivalent to softness in crime."[5]

STAGES IN CRIMINAL PROCEDURE

The National Commission on Law Observance and Enforcement has exposed the bare bones of criminal law administration. "Reduced to [their] lowest terms, the essentials of a criminal proceeding are (1) to bring the accused before or within the power of the tribunal, (2) a preliminary investigation to ensure that the crime is one that should be investigated, (3) notice to the accused of the offense charged, (4) opportunity to prepare for trial, procure witnesses, and make needed investigations, (5) a speedy trial, (6) a fair trial before an impartial tribunal, and (7) one review of the case as a whole by a suitable appellate interval. Criminal procedure should be as simple and direct as is consistent with these requirements."[6]

Prof. Herbert Wechsler has taken the position that, in the administration of criminal justice: "The two major procedural problems are those of apprehension and trial of the suspected persons."[7] The policeman is involved in the machinery of criminal justice with respect to both these functions. His role in the trial of a criminal case is generally limited to serving as a witness. However, the policeman occupies the center of the stage when the spotlight is directed toward the apprehension of the person suspected of perpetrating crime.

Obtaining Information

Many criminal prosecutions are initiated with little preliminary investigation, as may be the case when the act was done while the policeman was watching. He arrests the perpetrator immediately and takes down the names of those who saw the offense done. However, when substantial crimes have been perpetrated, or perhaps even some less substantial crimes, a complex apparatus of investigative machinery is brought into operation.

The quest for information concerning suspected crime is conducted on two separate levels. On one hand, interrogation is conducted in private by policemen, detectives, and prosecutors. On the other hand, interrogations may be conducted in a formal, prescribed way before the grand jury, under oath. There is a very important and substantial difference between the obtaining of information in the first category and in the second. The police and public prosecutor do not have the power to *compel* testimony, unless the person is first arrested, or to interrogate him under oath. The person questioned can refuse to answer the questions, without giving any explanation, and the law does not provide any punishment for such refusal.

Compare with this puny power of investigation that enjoyed by a grand jury, an examining judge, or a coroner. In these cases, the person summoned who is recalcitrant may be punished for his unwillingness to appear, to take an oath, or to answer proper questions asked him by an appropriate court through fine or imprisonment.

GRAND JURY

The most important institution with the power to compel testimony the grand jury. It is an agency that has a long history in our English legal system.

Originally it consisted of a panel of twenty-three citizens brought together for a county or district to deliberate for a certain period of time and to investigate alleged crimes within its territory. As a matter of practical operation today, it limits its deliberations to those matters that are presented for its consideration by the district attorney. It is only under extraordinary circumstances, when an irate public is clamoring that the public prosecutor's office is corrupt or otherwise derelict in its duties, that a "runaway" grand jury will act on its own initiative without regard to the direction of the prosecutor. It is the *prosecutor* who actually comes in to interrogate witnesses in the presence of the grand jury and acts in its name.

This type of formal interrogation has more value in investigating complex criminal events: stock frauds, income tax evasions, bribery of public officials, sophisticated schemes of fraud or extortion. In these situations, formal interrogation, coupled with the power to compel books and records to be produced, is very important. This procedure is less important in running down crimes of violence, of the sort with which the police are usually concerned.

A person accused of criminal conduct by the police or the public prosecutor must be taken before an examining judge within a short time after his arrest. A person called as a witness in the course of such investigation may be punished for willfully refusing to answer questions. However, the effectiveness of this preliminary investigation in producing valuable information is limited because of its formality, its limited purpose, and its narrow scope.

OTHER AGENCIES

It is worthy of note that the coroner is an official who has compulsory powers of investigation in the cases of suspicious deaths and, in some states, the case of unexplained fires. However, because the position is usually not full-time and because it requires medical rather than legal skill, the coroner generally does not enjoy an important role in the investigation of crimes.

In addition, in some jurisdictions there are other public officials who have the responsibility to investigate certain alleged crimes. Some are employed on a permanent, some on a temporary basis, and they have the right to carry on compulsory investigations.

The effectiveness of all of these procedures for investigating crime is restricted by the constitutional right of witnesses to refuse to answer questions that would tend to incriminate the person testifying.

POLICE AND PROSECUTOR

The police and the prosecutor do not have the legal authority compel anyone to appear for interrogation. Nor do they have authority to punish anyone for refusing to answer questions. Yet a p son who has been arrested or held in custody without being arres will usually find that, psychologically, it is almost impossible for h to stand mute. This is so even if he knows that he has the right remain silent. It is even more true, of course, if he is ignorant of rights. There are substantial restrictions on the power of the pol to hold a person without arresting him and also restrictions on t right of the police to arrest him.

ARREST

The sequence of events in a criminal case usually starts with t arrest of the accused person by the police. When the offense is a min one, this is followed by a trial. Where the charge is more serious, t complaint by the officer who made the arrest is not enough to institu a trial. Where there is such a serious offense, the arrest is followed a preliminary examination of the charges by a judge. The purpose this preliminary hearing is to decide whether the police or the distri attorney has furnished sufficient evidence to justify holding the accus person in custody or under bail pending formal accusation by t district attorney or the grand jury.

RELATION TO FORMAL ACCUSATION

In certain cases, the grand jury or the district attorney must tal formal steps before the arrest. Thus, in the federal system, if the Unite States Attorney decides to take action against a person who has n as yet been arrested, he may file an accusation against that person (information), charging a misdemeanor. Thereupon, the arrest is mad and the person charged either pleads guilty or faces trial without a opportunity for preliminary examination. If the offense charged is felony, the accusation (an indictment) can be made only by a gran jury. Once the indictment is filed, the person who is named in it arrested, and is held in custody or under bail to await trial. In th alternative, similarly, there is no preliminary investigation.

The legal authority of a prosecutor to file any information vari from state to state. In half the states, the public prosecutor may lodg an information for most felonies, as well as for misdemeanors, as the federal system. In almost all these jurisdictions, however, if th accused has not been arrested and afforded a preliminary investigation before a judge, the public prosecutor must have him arrested and taken before the examining judge for a preliminary examination. If the judge, upon his examination, does not find sufficient evidence to justify holding the suspect, in most states, the information may not be filed. In other states, the prosecutor may lodge an information for a misdemeanor, but only after authorization by the grand jury. However, as in the case in which the grand jury itself has made the indictment, the defendant does not have the right to preliminary examination after he is subsequently arrested.

In ancient times, the grand jury had the responsibility of presenting to the officials of the king, who rode the circuit, information about suspected crimes. The grand jurors, who were residents of the locality, had special knowledge of events occurring in the vicinity. The requirement that there be no trial for serious criminal offenses without an indictment by the grand jury (composed of one's neighbors), came to be regarded as a protection for individual citizens. This is what led to the rule that grand jury indictment was owed as a matter of constitutional protection. Today, the requirement of the grand jury indictment in only half the states shows that its importance is waning.

DETENTION WITHOUT ARREST

It is not essential to a criminal proceeding that there be an arrest. It is possible for a defendant to be arrested for the first time after he has been sentenced to prison. In the case of minor offenses, the defendant is summoned rather than arrested. If he fails to appear in court pursuant to the summons, he is then punished by the court.

Thus the whole scheme of criminal procedure puts a premium upon the policeman's knowledge of the various categories of criminal offenses—the felony, the misdemeanor, the offense. The precise classifications vary from jurisdiction to jurisdiction, but the factual categories are typical. All penal acts are misdemeanors, except felonies, which are punishable by death or imprisonment for more than a year. Misdemeanors with penalties of jail for six months or less, or fines of up to five hundred dollars, or both, are classified as petty offenses. The Supreme Court of the United States has held that the constitutional guarantee of a jury trial does not apply to a trial for a petty offense.

Preliminary Examination

In those cases where the charge against a suspect cannot be tried unless there has been an indictment or an information filed against him, if he has been arrested in advance of such information or indictment, he is entitled to a preliminary examination before a judge.

Under the law, the person so arrested must be taken before the judge promptly. What "promptly" means varies, depending upon the time of day or night when the arrest was made, possibly upon the day of the week, the distance between the place where the judge is holding court and the place of arrest, and other factors.

The basic purpose of the preliminary examination is to determine whether there appears to be sufficient evidence against the suspect to justify further criminal proceedings against him. As a practical matter, the examining judge does not make any effort to obtain evidence. Although the proceeding is called an "examination," it actually is not. Unless there is authority by statute, the examining judge or magistrate does not have the power to interrogate. The defendant is allowed to make a statement in his own behalf, if he wishes.

The examining judge does not determine the guilt or innocence of the defendant. If he decides that there is not sufficient evidence to justify further proceedings, he releases the defendant from custody or bail. If he concludes that the evidence is reasonably sufficient to bring about a conviction, he orders that the defendant be held for further proceedings. If the defendant is to be held for such further action, he is usually entitled to be released on bail.

FIRST AID FOR PERSON ARRESTED

The Association of the Bar of the City of New York and the New York Civil Liberties Union have prepared a pamphlet containing certain suggestions for a person who is arrested. While the law and the procedure vary from state to state, the advice given is helpful and worth following, in general.

On Arrest

The pamphlet suggests that, "if you are innocent," the following would apply:

What happens after you are arrested?

You are taken to a police station, where a record of your arrest and the charge against you must be reported without unnecessary delay in the "arrest book." Before questioning you, the police must tell you the charge. Where required by law, you will be fingerprinted and photographed.

Do you have to answer questions?

It is your right, under the Constitution, to refuse to say anything that may be used against you later—and to have the aid and advice of a lawyer at all times. After identifying yourself, you do **not** have to answer any questions or sign any paper about a crime. Neither a policeman nor anyone else may force you to do this. If any force or threats are used against you, report it to the District Attorney and to your own lawyer. You should also report promptly to the court any injuries and bruises suffered after arrest.

The promise of a policeman to help you or to intervene with the court, in exchange for a confession, is not binding.

Can you notify your family?

You are entitled to have one telephone call made within city limits, to tell your family, a friend, or your lawyer about your arrest. The police must do this promptly if you request it.

What happens to the money you may have with you?

You must be given an itemized receipt for all money and property taken from you when you are booked.

Can you be released on bail?

You have the right to be allowed to apply promptly for bail. Bail permits you to be released from jail, if an amount of money or other security is deposited with the proper official to make sure that you will appear in court. For some minor offenses, the police may release you on bail. In other cases, a judge fixes the amount of bail, and you have a right to be brought before him without unnecessary delay.

How can you get money for bail?

There are bail "brokers," licensed by the State of New York, who post a bond for bail (pay the amount for you). The fee they charge is regulated by the state. Charges are 5% on the first $1,000, 4% on the next $1,000 and 3% on the remaining sum. The minimum fee is $10. (Examples: $100 bond costs $10; $200, $10; $500, $25; $1,000, $50; $2,000, $90; $5,000. $180, etc).

In the Police Station

It advises the suspect of his rights in the police station:

What if you are innocent?

Even if you think you are not guilty, it is a crime to resist an officer who arrests you lawfully. Respect him. Do not talk back or be disorderly. If it turns out that you have been arrested illegally, you can sue the policeman for false arrest. But remember; if the arrest was a lawful one, the fact that you are innocent does not give you the right to collect damages. The following answers tell you how to get help to answer the charge and to protect your rights—whether you are innocent or not.

What can you be arrested for?

There are three kinds of violations for which you might be arrested. Felony is the name for the most serious violation. Less serious violations are called misdemeanors, and the least serious are known as offenses.

When can you be arrested?

A policeman may arrest you without a warrant:

1. If he sees you commit a violation of the law—or if he sees you try to commit one.

2. If someone committed a felony, and if the policeman has reason to believe you did it, even if he was not there at the time.

Must the policeman have a warrant?

In most situations a policeman must have a warrant to arrest you for a misdemeanor or an offense, if he did not see you do it himself. He does not need a warrant to arrest you for a felony.

What is a warrant?

A warrant is an order signed by a magistrate or a judge. It is made on a complaint by someone, and it charges that you committed a crime. The warrant must list the charges against you. It also must direct the policeman to make the arrest and to bring you before a magistrate or a judge. In the case of a misdemeanor, you cannot be arrested on a warrant on Sunday or at night unless the magistrate or judge says so in writing on the warrant itself. If a policeman has a warrant for your arrest, he must tell you he has it. You have the right to ask to see it. If you ask, he must show the warrant to you.

Can the policeman use force to arrest you?

If you resist a lawful arrest, the policeman can use all necessary force to arrest you. However, after you have been restrained, he cannot continue to use force.

An officer may break open a door or a window to make a lawful arrest or to serve a warrant, if you refuse to admit him.

In Court on Preliminary Examination

It advises the person being held in custody of his right in court.

When do you go before a magistrate?

After arrest and booking, you must be taken before a magistrate without unnecessary delay. If a magistrate is not then sitting in the right court, you may be held in a station house until the next court session.

Should you have a lawyer with you?

If possible, you should have a lawyer with you when you are taken before the magistrate. The magistrate must tell you the charge against you. He must inform you of your right to have a lawyer if you do not have one, and he must allow you a reasonable time to send for a lawyer if you do not have one. If you ask, he must put off the hearing so that you can get a lawyer. The magistrate must direct an officer to take a message to your lawyer, without a fee.

What if you cannot afford a lawyer?

If you are charged with a felony or a misdemeanor and you cannot pay for a lawyer, you can request legal aid. In the Court of Special

Sessions and the Court of General Sessions, the court must name a lawyer to defend you. In other courts, you may ask the magistrate if you are entitled to this assistance.

What does the magistrate decide?

The magistrate must hold a hearing at which witnesses are examined, and you have the right (but not the obligation) to testify. You can ask that that this hearing be adjourned until your lawyer can be present. For certain offenses, this hearing constitutes a trial so that the magistrate will dispose of the case directly and either dismiss the charge or find you guilty. In other cases, where he cannot try the charge himself, the magistrate decides only whether or not there is a reasonable basis for finding that you committed the offense charged. In such case you may waive the hearing. If you are charged with a misdemeanor, the magistrate will hold you for trial by the Court of Special Sessions: if it is a felony, he will hold you for the action of the Grand Jury.

What does the Grand Jury do?

The Grand Jury will either dismiss the charge against you or it will indict (accuse) you. If it indicts you, you must then stand trial in a trial court. You have a "right" to ask to appear before the Grand Jury when it is considering your case, but you should not make this request without the advice of your lawyer.

It suggests that the person in custody get a lawyer, that he say nothing that can be held against him, that he notify family or friends and apply for bail. He is advised not to resist a policeman, not to be disorderly or talk back, not to refuse entry for a lawful arrest. This advice is well taken.

The recent decision of the Supreme Court of the United States in the case of *Miranda* v. *Arizona*[8] adds weight to these suggestions. There, the Court, by a five-to-four vote, prohibited the questioning of a suspect being held in custody unless the person expressly waives his right to counsel or is actually being helped by an attorney.

However, as pointed out by Justice White in his dissent:

[The] decision leaves open such questions as whether the accused was in custody, whether his statements were spontaneous or the product of interrogation, whether the accused has effectively waived his rights, and whether non-testimonial evidence introduced at trial is the fruit of statements made during a prohibited interrogation, all of which is certain to be productive of uncertainty during investigation and litigation during prosecution. . . .

II.

Police Work and the Citizen

THE JOB SPECIFICATION *policeman* covers a tremendous range of functions. The police are primarily thought of as guardians of the safety of persons and property from malefactors in our homes and the street.

The policeman is trained to handle dangerous weapons and to chase and capture dangerous criminals. He is ready to assist lost children and the elderly or others who may need first aid. Today the policeman is made aware of the special problems of those who do not speak the language. He is able to handle crowds of people as well as vehicular traffic. Each policeman must digest a vast number of legal rules relating to the definition of crimes and evidence, and is expected to prepare elaborate forms and give testimony in court.

There is no country in the world which does not have a police force. In the United States, with its complex federal system, from the national government down to the smallest unit of local government, each level usually has its own police system.

What a Policeman Does

We generally have as our image of the policeman the man who regulates traffic and rides or walks up and down the streets. But the sphere of police work is constantly expanding to include the licensing of various trades and professions, the sale or possession of weapons, and the operation of places of public entertainment. The police frequently serve as inspectors or investigators. In such capacity, the policeman may look into the character or experience of a prospective licensee or applicant for employment by the government. He may have to decide whether a building is safe or pass on the morality of the inhabitants, evaluating whether public intervention is necessary. The police are sometimes given the job of public censorship and, in certain places, the administration of public assistance.

Patrol

For administrative and functional efficiency, generally the police departments are divided into specialized units. The basic unit is the patrol division. The patrolmen cover their "beats" either on foot or by motorcycle, automobile, or some other vehicle. They may employ men on horses or motorcycles for controlling crowds. And it is not uncommon for police to have patrols on rivers or near harbors. Most police cars are equipped with two-way radios so that they can be alerted to crimes, accidents, or disturbances very quickly. In New York City and elsewhere patrolmen keep in contact with the police headquarters by special telephones called "boxes," which are installed along the policeman's route. Use is being made of walkie-talkies. The patrolmen work in eight-hour shifts and as part of a squad. Each squad is led by a sergeant, and a number of squads are headed by a lieutenant.

Detective

In many places detectives are part of a detective division, which is broken up into various squads or bureaus. These bureaus or squads handle special types of criminal activity. Thus, the gambling squad investigates gambling; the dope squad investigates the use and sale of narcotics; the homicide squad looks into deaths under mysterious circumstances, or murders. Members of the detective division are often known as plainclothesmen because they wear their usual civilian clothes while investigating alleged crimes and they conceal their badges and weapons. The detective division is assisted by special services furnished by various chemical laboratories, ballistics experts, fingerprint experts, skilled photographers, and other persons who have special experience in crime detection. The Police Commissioner of New York City has proposed elimination of precinct detective squads entirely. He proposes to centralize the detective function, separating it out by specialty—rackets, narcotics, burglary, etc. Greater responsibility for the initial investigation would be delegated to the plainclothesmen at the precinct station house.

Traffic

Most of us encounter the policeman in connection with the direction of vehicular traffic. The traffic division, in addition, helps at school crossings, inspects automobiles to see that they meet licensing and safety standards, takes action against speeders and illegal parkers, and performs various other sundry and assorted jobs.

THE POLICEMAN AND THE PROSECUTOR

Modern government finds its sustenance in the raw data that i-
constantly fed it from many sources. It is this mass of informatior
from which the facts necessary to make judgments regarding publi
policy are derived. This material is gathered from routine physica
inspections, from examination of books and records that must be
kept as a condition precedent to doing business, and from many
other sources. And, in the administration of criminal justice, much
information is obtained in just this way. However, the procedure fo-
the investigation of specific alleged criminal offenses presents certair
problems worth considering.

It is not always realized that the agencies for such investigation are
of two sorts. The police and the district attorney constitute one type o
agency. The grand jury, the examining judge, and the coroner, armed
with the subpoena power and the legal authority to compel witnesses
to attend and testify, constitute the second type of agency. The investigation of specific crimes that have been perpetrated is for the
most part accomplished by the police and the public prosecutor.

In the United States, in investigating a specific alleged crime, the
office of the public prosecutor may either accept the facts that the
police are able to turn up or may disregard the efforts of the police
investigation. The prosecutor may make his own search for the evidence or may work together with the police, either in concert or on
a different avenue of inquiry.

At the local level, there is therefore a marked contrast in the
division of responsibility for the investigation of suspected crimes.
This may be a substantial problem, because there is no common
official to whom all investigating agents are required to respond.
The public prosecutor's office is usually a county agency; the police
department may be state-, city-, or village-operated. In addition, there
is often competition between the police department and the public
prosecutor for public support, funds, or political advantage. In the
major area of federal crime investigation, there is no such division of
responsibility. Any conflict that may exist is certainly very much less
intense in the federal system.

Two other factors are worthy of note. There is very little control
or supervision by the state over the local police or public prosecutor's
office, and there is a lack of integration of investigative services. Con-
comitantly, there is a need for adequate financing for these services.

Questioning of Persons in Custody

Although the police and public prosecutors lack the power to subpoena anyone, or to compel any person, arrested or not, to answer questions, they are still quite effective. It is almost impossible, psychologically speaking, to remain silent in the face of the brooding omnipresence of the law. Testimony comes from interested citizens, people who hate the suspect, informers who are seeking a reward or protection, or persons who believe, mistakenly, that they can be compelled to tell what they know.

When the wheels of a criminal proceeding start to roll, there are several stages during which the suspect may be kept in custody. If an arrest has been made before an indictment or if an information has been filed against the suspect, he may be held for the interval between the time of arrest and the time when he is brought before the examining judge. This period should be a short one, if the law is obeyed. The law itself specifies that the person held in custody be taken before a judge without delay. In large urban areas, there are examining judges available all day, each day of the week, and in some places even at night. In more sparsely settled areas, judges may not be readily available, so that, even without the intention of circumventing the law, a number of days may pass between the arrest and the preliminary examination.

Another period of detention may occur if the examining judge sets bail, pending action by the grand jury or the public prosecutor, and the suspect cannot furnish this bail. Or the crime may be one for which bail is usually not set, as in the charge of premeditated murder. If there is an indictment or an information filed and the suspect makes a plea of not guilty on the arraignment, he will be detained in custody until the end of the trial, unless he is let out on bail.

If this is a case in which the suspect is not arrested until after an indictment is made by the grand jury, the only periods of detention are the time between indictment and arrest and the short period between arrest and arraignment.

Release on bail is usually not obtained during the initial detention. The police, and perhaps the district attorney, have an opportunity to use this time to get the suspected person to make admissions or to confess, since the suspect may soon be released after he is taken before the judge.

The police and the prosecutor may interrogate the prisoner with scrupulous regard for the rights of the suspect. Or they may employ incessant questioning, extreme physical discomfort caused by lack of sleep or food, beatings, or subtle psychological pressures. For the latter practices, the label "third degree" is sometimes used. In 1931, a report submitted to the National Commission on Law Observance and Enforcement entitled, "Lawlessness in Law Enforcement," charged that resort to the third degree was widespread. The statement has been challenged by other authors.

During these periods of custody, the opportunities for the district attorney and the police to question the suspect vary, depending upon the conditions of detention. If the suspect is being held by a public official who is not actually connected with the police or the district attorney investigating the crime, the possibilities for the use of the third degree are fewer. Conversely, in an outlying area, where the sheriff who has custody of the prisoner also has the responsibility for controlling crime in the county and where he is a political associate of the district attorney, the conditions are more conducive to third-degree methods.

It should also be noted that, if the prisoner cannot be released on bail because he does not have the financial resources, which is most frequently the explanation, the indigent prisoner is certainly more amenable to interrogation by the police and the district attorney than his more affluent neighbor.

Another feature of police questioning of persons who have been arrested that is not sanctioned by the law is the "line-up." Persons who have been arrested for alleged serious crimes and who are not yet out on bail are lined up in the glare of a blinding light. They are subjected to the scrutiny of assembled detectives and to a bombardment of questions. A prisoner may refuse to answer, but, again, the situation is such that self-restraint is difficult.

In addition to interrogation during custody, the police may force the prisoner to submit to other procedures that may serve, during the detention, to his detriment as a human being. He may be required to put on or to take off articles of clothing; he may be asked to submit to physical examination or give blood samples. He may be asked to give a speciment of his handwriting, etc. And the admissions and confessions, fruits of this procedure, have usually been accepted by the courts, although it may be argued that they represent either a violation of the constitutional privilege against self-incrimination or an unreasonable search, as condemned by the United States Constitution and most state constitutions.

Use of the Period of Detention

The time between arrest and preliminary examination by the judge is a period during which the suspect most assuredly will be in custody. This is also the period during which the suspect is most vulnerable to confessing or making admissions. For this reason, police and prosecutors are under a strong temptation to extend this initial period of detention as long as is possible, without repercussions, when they are n the verge of obtaining an admission or a confession. There are nstances in which the police, in contravention of the legal require-nent of a preliminary examination before a judge, without delay, have eld suspects incommunicado for several days, or even longer, before ringing him before the court.

ORGANIZATION OF THE POLICE

A former Police Commissioner of New York City, Vincent L. Broderick, framed the question that underlies all police organization when he asked: "Who is to run the Police Department?" Every police department is subject to this problem—there are all sorts of competing pulls, competition within the department itself, and conflicting de-mands between civilian and police authority. Mayor John V. Lindsay gave the following answer:

> These desperate voices which have spoken in the past few weeks about the relationship between the Police Department and the Mayor have come perilously close to missing the basic principles of a democratically elected government. They have suggested—no, they have stated— that the Police Department is a law unto itself. They have stated that the duly elected civilian government of New York is not responsible for the Police Department as it is for the other departments in the city. The ultimate responsibility lies with the Mayor, and I intend to exercise that responsibility.

This is a good statement of democratic principle, but as Mayor Lindsay himself must realize, it is easier to state one's intentions than to carry them out, especially with regard to the police department. And, to the cop on the beat, the complex relationship between civilian authority and police operation, the ambiguities concerning the am-bivalences between his private and official views must fill him with doubts and frustrations.

Centralized Systems

As the problem of organization of the police is world-wide, there are a number of different solutions in existence. Most European police systems, and those in other areas of the world, are centralized. In such a system, there is one official, part of the national government, who is the chief executive for all matters of police control and manage-ment. Even where a local unit of government and a police district cover the same geographic area, the national police official still has the final say. In France the central body is called the *Sureté nationale.* A policeman is known as an *agent.* In smaller towns and rural areas, the *gendarmerie,* or military police, conduct police affairs. In Italy, the *carabinieri* are the uniformed police, and the *sicurezza pubblica* refers to the plainclothes detectives.

In totalitarian countries, a good deal of the work of the police is in weeding out political heresy. Such police systems have a central secret-police agency, with agents and spies who ferret out subversives and disloyal persons. The Russian czars maintained a secret police called the *Cheka;* after the Russian revolution this work was carried on for the national government by the Ogpu, the NKVD, and the MVD. At the present time, in the Soviet Union, the work is done by the MVD and the KGB. The Nazis in Hitler's Germany used the terror-striking Gestapo.

Interpol, the International Police Commission, serves as an information-exchange agency and a center for cooperation among most European police systems.

Partially Decentralized Systems

The second type of police system is partially decentralized. The best example of such a police organization exists in England. There, the British Home Office supervises the local police through a staff of Inspectors of Constabulary. The national government also gives financial assistance to the local police forces. There are approximately 150 local police units, which answer to a local government authority. If any local police agency is not operating properly, the national subsidy is stopped. The head of a police department, the Chief Constable, may ask help from the London Metropolitan Police. The London Metropolitan Police has its office in New Scotland Yard. "Scotland Yard" is the name often used for the criminal investigation department of the London Metropolitan Police.

Decentralized Systems

Last, there is the police system such as exists in the United States and Canada. This is a decentralized system in which all levels of government maintain virtually independent systems. The result is often overlapping and causes confusion. There is no central police agency, but there is cooperation in the exchange of information regarding criminals and crime statistics. Radio and teletype facilities are used extensively throughout the country for this cooperative effort.

LOCAL POLICE

The size of the local police force ranges from a force with a single policeman to one with approximately thirty thousand men and women, as in New York City. It has been suggested by experts that a well-organized police agency should have available one policeman for every two thousand residents in the area. In large towns or in cities, the force may be divided into districts or precincts, each with its own station house. In smaller communities, the operation of the police force may be centered in a single police headquarters building. There is considerable similarity in the police table of organization in different localities. The head of the force may be titled commanding captain, chief, superintendent, commissioner or director. There is a distinction between commissioned and noncommissioned personnel, as in the army. The subordinate officers are generally deputies, inspectors, captains, lieutenants, and sergeants.

COUNTY POLICE

The county police force extends throughout a county, except for towns and cities. The head law-enforcement officer in the county is usually known as the sheriff. He has the responsibility for the county jail facilities and the custody and care of its inmates. His staff of policemen are known as deputies, and their number ranges from hundreds to a single member. The sheriff's office is still the main police agency in the western and southern parts of the United States.

FEDERAL AND STATE INVESTIGATIVE (POLICE) AGENCIES

In the United States, the federal police agencies enforce the many penal laws. More and more, they work closely with the various state, county, and local police. The most important federal police agencies are the Federal Bureau of Investigation (FBI), the Border Patrol, and the Bureau of Narcotics and Dangerous Drugs in the Department of Justice, the Bureau of the Chief Postal Inspector in the Post Office Department, the United States Secret Service, the Internal Revenue Service, the Alcohol Tax Unit, the Bureau of Customs, and the United States Coast Guard in the Department of the Treasury.

Under federal law, the jurisdiction and scope of authority of each federal agency is defined and limited. They do not have power to enforce state laws. Yet, within the states, they may make arrests for violations of federal law, such as income tax evasions.

The nine agencies mentioned are not the sole police systems of the federal government. In addition, there are such agencies as the Department of State (passport and extradition laws), the National Park Service (forest preservation), the Public Health Service (control of epidemic diseases), the Department of Agriculture (animal and plant quarantine), as well as others.

HISTORY OF THE POLICE

The English origins of the present-day police system go back to the Anglo-Saxon organization of communities for security purposes into tens, tithings, and hundreds. About 800 A.D., each ten families made up a tithing and chose their representative. Ten tithings constituted a "hundred" and elected a reeve as their head. A number of hundreds made up a county or shire. The term "sheriff" is derived from the title shire reeve. When the Normans came in with William the Conqueror in 1066, this system of maintaining law and order was continued. All men capable of doing so were required to join in the "hue and cry" in the pursuit of a criminal suspect. "Watch and ward" duty was required from all able-bodied men over sixteen years of age. These men put down disturbances, detained suspicious persons, and interrogated strangers caught after dark.

As urban life developed, the police system became more organized and complex. By the nineteenth century, London had set up its own night watch and had special police patrols to guard the business places, wharves, and other areas. A group of police agents, the "Bow Street Runners," served legal papers for the courts. The Metropolitan Police of London, a body of professional policeman, was organized in 1829 by Sir Robert Peel. The nickname "bobbies" or "peelers" was applied to them in honor of the founder, and the name has persisted till today.

Because of their own experience, the colonists from England brought along with them the watch and ward system. The men who served were generally unpaid volunteers, except where wealthy or influential people hired special guards.

In the nineteenth century, Boston established a professional police force of six men. By the middle of the past century, New York had created an eight-hundred-man force for work during the day. By 1870, cities and towns throughout the United States had police forces. In 1919, the Boston police went on strike when the police commissioner refused to permit them to join labor unions.

At the end of the nineteenth century, policemen were termed constables. It has been suggested that the word "cop" is a contraction for c.o.p., which meant constable on patrol. Another theory is that "cop" is a shortened form of "copper," a term applied to the star-shaped badge of copper worn by a policeman, hence for the policeman himself.

POLICE WORK AS A CAREER

Most police forces now operate under civil service status, and the members must pass civil service examinations. Pensions and sick leaves are almost universal. The jobs can be terminated usually only "for cause" after a hearing, once the policeman has completed his probationary period. The disadvantages of being a policeman are the danger, long hours, and the relatively low pay.

The requirements for appointment vary, but they all include good physical condition and good character. Most departments investigate applicants very carefully with respect to background. Almost every police force requires a high school diploma, and many federal agencies require college training. The age requirements generally range between twenty-one and thirty-two with the physical requirements similar to those set by the armed forces.

It seems noteworthy that the New York City Police Department has undertaken a program to recruit and prepare young men from low-income areas in the city to make them eligible for police careers. This step should increase the reservoir of available manpower. At the same time, it should strengthen the relationship of the police department with the minority groups, who to an important degree make up the poor. This program is being undertaken by the Department in cooperation with the Board of Education and the Manpower Training Program, which is financed by the federal government.

Promotion requires a consistently good record and intelligence. Detectives in New York City now get additional training at the Police Academy before beginning their duties. Detectives are often selected on the basis of an examination. It has been suggested, however, that direct recruitment for the detective division might be worth trying, since investigative ability is not of the same order as the skills required for other types of police work. Yet, time spent as a patrolman has great value for a detective-to-be.

One cannot help but be impressed by the wide range of skills and the years of training that must go into molding a capable policeman. Yet the one message that emerges loud and clear from observations of police work has been stated by Thomas R. Brooks:

> The police cannot do everything. They can solve crimes. Police presence, on foot, on scooter or in a patrol car, can discourage crime at one particular moment in one particular place. But the police cannot be everwhere at once—and this would probably be an intolerable city if that were possible.[1]

Actually, a serious question exists as to the extent to which police activity does affect the crime rate. The Superintendent of Police of Chicago, O. W. Wilson, has observed:

There are many crime causes, such as slum conditions, narcotics addiction, lack of parental responsibility, unemployment, cultural inequalities and other social factors over which the police have no influence or control.[2]

There is a growing awareness that the control of crime is dependent upon many factors other than traditional police work. A report of the President's Commission on Law Enforcement and Administration of Justice,[3] issued in February 1967, has warned that the country can "expect increased amounts of reported crime" for the next several years.

Nicholas de B. Katzenbach, former Attorney-General and chairman of the Commission, gave these reasons to support this prediction:

(1) The unusually large percentage of the population in its teens and early twenties, "the high risk ages for involvement in crime."

(2) "Greatly increased concentration of our population in the cities where crime rates have usually been highest."

(3) "Increased opportunities for crime which come with increased affluence."

(4) "The growing sense of deprivation and frustration of segregated minority group members who are keenly aware of the opportunities of an affluent society, but are denied access to them."

(5) The proportion of the reported crime increase which is due to better reporting methods.

A study of professional crime in New York, Chicago, Atlanta, and San Francisco has shown that the operational procedures of the courts "tend to increase, rather than decrease, the over-all amount of crime that professional criminals commit." Bail costs, lawyers' fees, and other expenses that are assumed by the typical professional criminal who wishes to stay out of prison during the usually lengthy period between his arrest and final disposition of his case "increase the pressures for him to engage in crime while free."[4] One of the major conclusions of this study was that detectives spend too much of their time in activities that are "essentially irrelevant to crime control."

The complexity of the burden that is thrust upon the police is further emphasized by the fact that most crimes may not be committed for gain or even by professional criminals. At a recent convention of the American Psychological Association,[5] it was reported that factors such as personality conflicts between marital partners, sexual and emotional disorders, and societal pressures contribute to a startling number of crimes. For example, it was brought out that almost 38 per cent of all homicides in the United States take place within the family. In addition, in 40 per cent of all homicides in this country, the murderer and the victim were friends.

III.

The Policeman in Society

IT IS COMMONPLACE to criticize the police when a crime is committed. What is frequently overlooked is that the policeman is only one of the instruments for controlling antisocial conduct, and by no means the most important. Even superficial reflection verifies this conclusion. If concentration of police could guarantee low crime rate, then the areas with the highest police density would enjoy the least amount of crime. Yet, this does not appear to be the case.

Social control is determined by the degree to which people conform to an established form of behavior. Most people who obey the law are for the most part not thinking of the policeman at all. They are responding to built-in conditioning, which is enforced and reinforced by social pressures, such as parental or peer-group approval or disapproval, gossip, recognition as an individual, and by a whole web of community institutions that generate such pressures. The policeman is far down on the list of effective molders of social behavior.

In smaller countries with slower-changing cultures, where the people are more united in beliefs, customs, and attitudes and where life is simpler, there is generally little need to call upon the police to maintain order. There is less of a need for jails or mental institutions, since aberrant conduct can be handled by the existing social structures within the community. Since everyone knows everyone else and is dependent upon everyone else, public esteem is very important, and this inhibits conduct that would occasion disapproval. In such a society, young people grow up knowing their respective roles and they learn the uniformly held set of values as to what is right or wrong. If there is a person who serves as a policeman, he is supported by the fact that he is enforcing legal standards that are also moral ones, accepted by the community.

In a speech delivered a few years ago, former Police Commissioner of New York, Michael J. Murphy, acknowledged the changing nature of police work.

> The nature of police work in a modern society has changed dramatically. It is no longer a matter of cops and robbers alone. It has become more a question of people and police, and the police have found themselves drawn into many problems, many grievances, for which they are not responsible and which they, as police, cannot solve.
>
> In the last few years, the police departments in all cities in this nation have found themselves confronted with and drawn into the battle for equal rights. They have found themselves in the no man's land of the battle and the recipients of the fire of both sides. Yet, if they are to do their job properly, they must continue to remain in that position in order to carry out their sworn duties to protect the peace.

This change in the nature of police work is a resultant of a society that is undergoing radical changes in its economic, political, technological, and moral systems (and all at the same time). People are changing their relationships to one another, some are ascending the socioeconomic ladder, some are going down. New persons and groups are attaining political power; some are enjoying new economic rewards. These benefits are usually being seized by those who are ready to disregard or destroy the established order. And the ongoing economic, political, and technological revolutions reinforce those who challenge the old order. One of the universal concomitants of such upheaval is the breakdown in the social homogeneity of the community.

Historically, this sort of displacement has always been accompanied by an increase in crime. The community, in its anxiety, often resorts to legal rules and sanctions to maintain peace and order. It is easy to blame the policeman (since one must have a scapegoat) if he cannot bring back the "good old days." Certainly, this analysis has some relevance for our time and our place.

"Enforcing the Unenforceable"

The job of the police today has been described as "enforcing the unenforceable." Mayor John V. Lindsay of New York City appointed a Law Enforcement Task Force, which, in a recent report, recognizes the magnitude of this problem. It is expected that the police enforce the laws with respect to a wide range of proscribed activities, including such diverse offenses as working on Sunday, walking on the grass in parks, and jay-walking. Attempts to enforce such regulations, which are often disregarded, create antagonisms between the police and the citizenry by blanketing them in "the tolerance of widespread disrespect for the law, for example, parking offenses." It breaks down morale, said the Task Force, to have an assignment that cannot be carried out, particularly if the community does not really expect to have it effectively performed. In these situations, "if a police officer takes action, he appears as a hostile force acting in opposition to the community; if he withholds action, he encourages disrespect for the law and exposes himself to suspicion of corruption."

The policeman's job is essentially that of keeping the peace rather than enforcing the law. Actually, what is required is that the officer be available—available for emergencies and to render all kinds of assistance to those who require aid. Citizens demand more and more arrests of muggers, rapists, murderers, drug pushers, but police coverage is not sufficient for that, nor would more arrests solve the crime problem. During his eight hours of pounding the beat (with time off for lunch) the patrolman is collecting information to relay back to headquarters and he is using his good offices and authority to resolve the difficulties that arise in the street without resort to detention or arrest of the individuals involved.

The law does not expressly give the policeman discretion to decide whether or not to enforce its provisions, but the public accepts such exercise of discretion. The traffic cop may or may not give the driver a summons because the car's tail light did not work, depending upon how the "story" of the motorist affected him. This gives the policeman tremendous social, moral, and administrative power. The way that this discretion is exercised depends upon a number of variables. In some areas, the police may be less strict with respect to gambling or assaults or loitering, in other places more strict. The policeman may be influenced in his decisions by the "class" of people involved or by the nature of the alleged offense. The policeman may be more strict with recognized criminals or with those segments of the population that he considers a greater threat to the police than others.

The policeman may not act because he has not mastered all the intricacies of the increasingly complex criminal law, or it may be that he cannot keep up with its volume. And he is often inhibited by the fact that he may be liable to civil damages or administrative penalties if he makes a mistake. He may be affected by the social standing of the persons involved, or by a special relationship that one of the people has with the police or with a political power. He will be influenced by the folkways and mores of the neighborhood in which he works. His legal obligation may be tempered by the need to maintain a good relationship with the people who live on his beat.

It is noteworthy that, when they take action, the police seem to emphasize the moral aspect of their conduct rather than the letter of the law. The policeman often tries to urge a change in conduct or even to convince a malefactor that he, the policeman, is morally right in making an arrest. Perhaps part of the reason why so relatively few people are arrested is that the policeman's moral code and the letter of the law do not always coincide. Obviously, standards of police morality and conduct fluctuate. A generation ago, a deftly wielded night stick was a socially approved method of maintaining order. Today, the restrictions on police action, dictated by public morality, are more stringent. The public has limited the scope of discretion once enjoyed by the policeman with respect to police action.

There are very few professions or occupations in which the spectrum of problems or social relationships is as varied as that to which the policeman is exposed. Policemen, often young, inexperienced in life situations, limited in academic background, are called upon to deal with all types of emotion-wrought people. Gradually, most of them learn to cope with this wide range of problems, perhaps not consciously, but on an experiential basis. Policemen develop invisible antennae that adjust automatically to relate to "upper-class" people and to "lower-class" people.

The policeman himself may not be aware that he is making such a distinction, but his manner, his speech, his way of confronting a situation will usually vary depending on his social evaluation. It is true that a policeman should function without respect to class—all persons should be treated the same way. But, realistically, it is as difficult for a policeman to step away from the social situation as a picture from its frame. Unfortunately, if the policeman has encountered difficulty with members of one social group, rather than another, he is liable to categorize the entire group as trouble-makers. Of course, what constitutes "trouble" to a policeman depends to a considerable extent upon his own social, political, and economic predilections. Thus, a policeman, prejudiced against Mexicans, may approach an area where Mexicans reside with a predisposition to find trouble.

"But Don't Get Caught"

In a society in which the ethics of the market place are "don't get caught!", the policeman, a member of the same society, is as vulnerable as anyone. The temptations of the affluent America are difficult to resist, especially since the rewards of dishonesty may be very high. Unfortunately, belief in police corruption is shared alike by the citizen in the ghetto and the citizen in the luxury apartment on the East Side. The actual dishonest act may be picayune, nothing more than a bag of groceries from a grocer who wishes to show his thanks to a policeman who has thwarted a robbery or headed off an obnoxious drunk. As one former Deputy Police Commissioner put it: "You get a peculiar rationalization about [clean money] and dirty money." Shaking down a prostitute or narcotics peddler is one thing, but taking money from a merchant who wishes to remain open for business on Sunday may be considered to be in another category.

Violence and Civil Rights

The media of communication and mass entertainment focus on the violence in American life. Remember that violence is part and parcel of the American tradition, engendered through myth, boyhood stories and games, and historic folklore. This fact must have a significant impact on the readiness of criminals to resort to violence, with the resultant greater risk to the policeman on the beat. And, of course, the policemen themselves are products of the same tradition.

The policeman does work that is tension-provoking because, while it is usually plodding and dull, he stands at the edge of a volcano that may erupt at any moment into violence. He knows that he must be prepared to use force to do his job—to protect himself. He is trained to use his revolver, something that he may never have to do, yet he must always be ready, psychologically and physically, to draw first and perhaps kill. That gun is part of the policeman's life. New York Commissioner Murphy is alleged to have said, on the day he resigned from the New York City Police Department: "I'll keep this [his gun]. I'll feel undressed without the thing. When you get up in the morning, it's like putting on your tie."

One of the serious ambivalences of the policeman's life is that on one hand he is by temperament and training accustomed to taking orders, to conforming to semimilitary discipline, to doing his work "by the numbers," according to the manual. On the other hand, his work, every day, requires initiative and independence. An example of the dilemma that confronts the policemen is expressed in the words of a working detective:

"The mouthpiece will take a month to get ready to come to court and then ask for six adjournments. The trial judge will stew over his decision for weeks. A joker like me has to decide in a split second. Will he come at me with a knife? Will he take a shot at me with a gun? Should I swing at him? Where should I hit him? If I hit him too easy, he may finish me, first! If I slug him too hard, he may sue me or file a complaint."

The police cannot really be effective if they do not get cooperation from the public. If minority groups are suspicious about police attitudes toward them and are in fear of physical violence at the hands of the police, the value of the police department is in serious jeopardy

It is possible, perhaps probable, that claims of police brutality are exaggerated. But claims of such violence occur and reoccur. For in stance, consider the story of Horace Cates. On March 17, 1961, Mr Cates, a hospital laboratory technician, says he looked through the window of his home and saw a cluster of white youngsters throwing bricks at his automobile. He says that they chanted, "Nigger, nigger come on out."

He came out and called to a police officer who was standing at the corner. He complained, and the hoodlums attacked him. Instead of helping him, Mr. Cates charged, the policeman held him, permitting one of the youths to hit him on the head with an iron pipe. The wound required fourteen stitches. "Then," Mr. Cates said, "additional police finally arrived at the place of the incident, but they did not stop the attack." He himself was arrested and charged with unlawful assembly.

Former Deputy Police Commissioner Walter Arm has complained that during his tenure the standing of the New York City Police Department was unfairly criticized, because "the New York City pa-trolman was automatically equated with the red-necked sheriff; and the New York Department was criticized for the use of police dogs and fire hoses in the South, although no such measures were ever employed —or thought of— in our City."

The Deputy Commissioner's observations may be accurate, but he has missed an important factor in the relationship between the police and minority groups. Minority groups frequently lack confidence in the willingness of the police to give protection to their communities. Even enlightened and high-ranking police officers seem to lose sight of this fact. Thus, when former New York City Police Commissioner Vincent L. Broderick declared that "there is some considerable con-fidence in civil rights circles in the present leadership of the Police Department," the comment of the Chairman of the Harlem chapter of the Congress of Racial Equality was: "He's out of his cotton-picking mind." Yet one of former Commissioner Broderick's last official acts was to dismiss Patrolman William F. Whitehead, twenty-seven years old, who was charged with having beaten a Negro merchant seaman with a revolver while searching him for narcotics on October 10, 1964. The charges stated that the patrolman did not arrest the man, did not get him medical attention, and did not report the event. It was the seaman who made the report. While spokesmen for the police point to such disciplinary action as proof of their position that the police are impartial, they ignore the significant fact that the nonwhite com-munity in America, and many segments of the white communities, feel that brutality does exist. This hurts the cause of law enforcement.

Private Police Attitudes and Public Policy

In spite of the efforts of the top echelons in many police departments to bring about a change, there still appears to exist considerable resentment among policemen against minority groups. Thomas R. Brooks, in an article in *Commentary,* describes a bull session he attended at the Police Academy, conducted by a representative of the New York City Human Rights Commission and attended by a class of recruits. The recruits did not disguise their conviction that the spiel was being made because "It's in his book," or that "He's getting paid to say that." The men apparently accepted many of the stereotypes of prejudice. "Property depreciates when the colored move in. We have this supposed great welfare state; we give 'em money . . . this an' that, but it doesn't seem to do any good . . . It seems like a waste of money. We're building new slums for them, that's all . . . How can a place get filthy, unless you put filth in it?" And so it went.[1]

The policeman derives his attitudes from a number of different sources. He absorbs the extent of his public obligation from his supervisors and those with whom he works, and finds out what is expected of him from the citizens with whom he comes in contact. If his boss has lax attitudes about payola, it will not be too difficult to have his views rub off on the susceptible patrolman.

If the building contractors, time after time, offer him a few bucks to "look the other way" because the sidewalk is obstructed, he may finally succumb, even if his intentions were good initially. If the courts make arrests more and more difficult because of the strict and complex requirements that their decisions lay down, this may make the policeman more careful. It may also make for fewer arrests. But, perhaps more significantly, the policeman brings with him to the job, in and out of uniform, his own social experience. In addition to his service revolver and other paraphernalia, the police officer carries with him a built-in value system, molded by his own life experiences. He can carry out public policy only after it is filtered through these social values following his own unconscious psychological motivations.

The role of policeman and its terms and conditions of employment attract a certain sort of person. The job offers an opportunity for a young man in the economic lower class to rise a rung or two in the American hierarchy of success. It also affords some measure of financial security. And, of course, it is attractive to certain personality types. The policeman usually finds it easy to conform to the red tape of civil service requirements. He is generally comfortable within a military structure and discipline. Most police forces are organized on a quasi-military basis, and, as one would expect, most policemen are veterans of the armed forces. Many young men, discharged from the service after Korea or World War II, having little or no interest in the scholarly or business life, and attracted by the economic advantages, have "found a home" in the police forces of America.

A commentator on the conflict between the demands of the shifting attitudes of society and the policeman's values, has put it this way:

> Many of the changes taking place offend the lower-middle-class morality which generally prevails among policemen and which is of the same order as the morality Mr. Doolittle vainly inveigled against. Cops are conventional people. Only recently a patrolman was dismissed from the force because his wife won an annulment on the grounds that he refused to have relations with her; another (unmarried) was fired because he had been having sexual relations with a woman not his wife (also unmarried), which 'tended to cause criticism detrimental to the department.' Tolerance is not a police virtue: all a cop can swing in a milieu of marijuana smokers, interracial dates, and homosexuals is the night stick. A policeman who passed a Lower East Side art gallery filled with paintings of what appeared to be female genitalia could think of doing only one thing—step in and make an arrest. . . .[2]

This imposes a tremendous burden on the man on the beat. Ex-Mayor Robert F. Wagner of New York City advised a batch of new police recruits: "You are not really supposed to be human nor to have fears or frailties of your own. This is part of the responsibilities you will bear." This substantial burden of responsibilities inhibits the execution of public policy by the police.

Police Participation in Civic Affairs

Historically, the police department, and the members of the department themselves, have been part and parcel of political matters. There are a number of reasons for this state of affairs. Frequently, chief of police is an elective position, and, even more frequently, the person who appoints the police chief is an elected official. Yet there has always been a countervailing theme in police administration: that the policeman himself remain aloof from politics in carrying on his public responsibilities, since law enforcement must be conducted without favor or prejudice. Certainly, the trend has been to divorce the police function from politics. Today, when the cop talks about the importance of "influence," he is generally referring to contacts within the department rather than the kind of political influence that was once necessary for appointment or promotion.

The debate on the relation of the police to politics brings to mind an opinion written by Justice Holmes when he was still a young judge sitting in the Massachusetts Supreme Court, concerning a police regulation in New Bedford, which forbade any policeman to raise money for political purposes.[3] When officer McAuliffe was fired from the force for doing exactly that, he pleaded that the rule had invaded his constitutional right to express his political opinions. Holmes' rejoinder was sharp and direct: "The petitioner may have a right to talk politics, but he has no constitutional right to be a policeman."

In New York City, police department rules provide that: "A member of the force shall not affiliate with or become a member of any organization if such affiliation or membership would in any way interfere with or prevent him from performing police duty." Another departmental regulation gives a policeman the right to vote, to entertain political or partisan opinions, and to express them freely when they do not concern the immediate discharge of his duties. Police Commissioner Howard R. Leary has stated that policemen may belong to the John Birch Society if membership does not "impair their efficiency." In Chicago, a police department representative noted that police are not permitted to engage in social or organizational activities that are inimical to the best interests of the country. He also pointed out that they could not belong to "any organization which recommends or advocates anything but a democratic way of life. Whether this interpretation would cover the John Birch Society has not come up." In Santa Ana, California, Police Chief Edward J. Allen reported that participation in "subversive or even partisan political organizations" was barred, "but we have no proof that John Birch Society members fall into that category." That particular police department was shaken in November of 1964, when Allen ousted a police officer on the charge that the Birchers were attempting to take over the leadership of the local police benevolent association.

A spokesman for the Boston police department reported that the police membership in the John Birch Society has "just not become an issue." He explained that the only restriction was on joining labor organizations. In Nassau County, New York, policemen are not permitted to join "any group that is either subversive or political." "We have never bothered to check whether they are members [of the John Birch Society]," the spokesman advised. "If you prohibit membership in the John Birch Society, you have to prohibit membership in other groups. I don't know where you'd draw the line." In other parts of New York State, similar views were expressed.

The Police Commissioner of White Plains, New York, agreed. He also added that a regulation that police not "belong to secret organizations or groups which advocated overthrow of the government would not seem to apply to the Birch Society."

"I don't known how to classify it, but it can't be secret because it has offices. There's even one here in White Plains." The Commissioner went on to say that a police officer could belong to the Birch Society, "providing he did the job for which he was hired, which is to enforce the law and keep the peace to the same degree for anyone and everyone."[4]

Alienation of the Police from the Rest of the Community

"Policemen," pointed out H. L. Mencken, "enjoy a social life almost as inbred as that of the Justices of the United States." And perhaps for many of the same reasons. A former Police Commissioner has expressed it this way:

"We had a series of events that caused the public to come in contact with the police in an unusual context—to see a community of interest with the police, rather than the usual antagonism. You know, ordinarily the policeman lives in a world of his own. There's a barrier between him and the rest of humanity, and, as a result, he's much happier when he's dealing with other policemen. He becomes isolated. If there's one reason police morale is comparatively high now, it's because of these events that brought the police and the public together." [5]

For the most part, policemen are quite a cohesive group, showing sympathy with each other's problems and dangers. There are many reasons for this attitude. They feel that by virtue of their positions, they encounter more threats, physical violence, and risk of death than members of most other vocations. The policeman may be legally held accountable for acts that result in erroneous arrest, injury, or property damage. All this helps to create a feeling of mutual dependence among police officers, and one of group solidarity. This group feeling seems to spill over into other areas than the usual police routine, extending to such matters as family concerns and political philosophy. The feeling increases when policemen go on patrol, either on foot or in cars, in pairs. One member of the team may cover up an illegal or undesirable act of his buddy, even from the police higher-ups. This provides greater protection for the individual policeman, but makes for separation from the rest of the population.

Such solidarity may have some other pernicious effects as well. When the police position is held by the entire law-enforcement group, and this position is not shared by or is antagonistic to that held by the community at large, greater hostility develops between the public and the police.

A complaint universally held by police officers is that they are not supported by the courts and the public to the extent to which they should be. Many complain that the emphasis on civil rights has ignored the importance of civil responsibilities. And they feel angered by the decisions of the Supreme Court of the United States in recent years, which restrict the attempts of policemen to deal with criminals. "The police," says Michael J. Murphy, former Commissioner of the Police Department of New York, "are being subjected to unfair abuse and undeserved criticism from some quarters in what I can only regard as a planned pattern of attack to destroy effectiveness and to leave the city open to confusion. . . ." He continues:

> For the ironic truth of the matter is that the police officer, too, belongs to a minority group, a highly visible minority group—and is also subject to stereotyping and mass attack. Yet he, like every member of every minority, is entitled to be judged as an individual and on the basis of his individual acts, and not as a group.
> But this is not happening. At the present time, the police are being attacked unfairly and bearing the brunt of a campaign of mass libel. Scattered and isolated acts are being used to label all police-men as bullies and brutes, and this mass attack is being launched to discourage impartial police action, to damage the police reputa-tion and to dilute the effectiveness of the Police Department.[6]

That the policemen are not being paranoidal in feeling that their efforts are not appreciated may be easily documented. As Pete Hamill recently wrote in his column in the New York *Post:*

> People grow up in places like Harlem, Bedford-Stuyvesant and Red Hook with a notion of the Cop-as-Bogeyman. The cop is the abstraction small children are threatened with and in most situations the reactions is so built in that a riot, a brick-throwing party or a simple assault can happen faster than any group of citizens in this town could be reached by telephone.[7]

The nature of a policeman's life, out of uniform, does not sub-stantially strengthen his ties with the rest of the community. While on duty, the policeman must condition himself not to inject his private personality into the performance of his job. But the policeman in America is considered to be on duty twenty-four hours a day, seven days a week. As a consequence, he is always on "good behavior." He cannot entirely give himself to his own interests and his own life. His friends always feel the shadow of the policeman's official position darkening their relationship. The officer's personal life is hedged with restrictions as to associations and activities. These limitations are designed to restrict him from corruption, compromising situations, or the appearance of either. He is at the call of neighbors, more than other persons, much as a physician is. Obviously, his friends and associates must be chosen with care.

All these factors contribute to the sense of isolation that policeman feel in varying degrees. This feeling of separateness permeates the entire life of the policeman, extending even to his relationship with his wife and children.

The Social Nature of Police Administration

It is difficult to evaluate the efficiency of a police department in carrying on its work because in so doing a number of criteria must be satisfied. It is not enough to rid the streets of criminals: the department must operate so that the innocent are protected. In a democratic society, the police have the obligation of reflecting the entire community and they cannot operate effectively unless they reflect the entire community.

In England and the United States, the role of the policeman is that of an ordinary citizen who is given special legal authority in order to perform his job. As the police take on more and more specialized responsibilities, this simplistic conception of the job of a policeman becomes more difficult to continue. Yet, the idea that each policeman is a nursemaid to society and that he can handle any sort of trouble is still widely prevalent.

The basic pattern of the police administrative organization supports this analysis. Aside from a few specialists in laboratories, and others, as we go up the promotional line, the sergeant, the inspector, the captain are regarded as patrolmen who have taken on additional (but not really different) responsibilities with each promotion. The qualifications are considered different in quantity but not in quality.

The job description is geared to the rendering of personal service, not necessarily at the dictate of the persons served. The policemen rely upon their own evaluations of what the situation demands, in the light of what the officer, himself, evaluates that the public good dictates.

Some of the ambiguity of the status of the policeman in our society, some of the uncertainty of his role and the ambivalence about his own professionalism, are reflected in the problem presented by James F. Bale, Chief of Police of Whittier, California:

Do the men of your department receive free coffee, meals at half price, 10 per cent discount at department stores, candy, cigars, and other "gifts" at Christmastime? These gratuities, unfortunately, have been viewed as acceptable "fringe benefits" to law enforcement careers in some areas. I am sure that there are many in the police profession, who see nothing wrong with a grateful businessman's expressing his heartfelt appreciation to the local police department by presenting something free, or at least a discount on items purchased at his establishment. I would suggest that this has no place in the development of law enforcement as a truly recognized profession.

. . . Do you carefully recruit, select and train your police officers? Do you instill in them a sense of pride, and uniform them with the badge of honor worn proudly over their heart? And then, do you send them into the marketplace to say, "Brother, can you spare a dime?" [8]

Life is becoming increasingly impersonal and complex. The policeman's work seems to be less and less based on personal relationship with people in the community and more and more on specialized police skills and nonpolice controls. This makes police work more difficult. Attempts should be made to support a closer policeman-citizen relationship. Public relations is important but it is only one facet of dealing with the problem. It is important to maintain police morale and a feeling by the policeman that his work is meaningful. The citizen must recognize that the policeman cares and that he can render the services that are needed. The optimum relationship between the policeman and the citizen will come about if the private role of the policeman and his public one become closely identified. This may not be easy, as most present-day pressures are in the opposite direction.

The Chief Inspector of the New York Police Department, Sanford Garelik, has put the solution in these terms: "The police must become part of the community, not just 'we' and 'they,' but 'us.' "

IV.

The Constitution in the Police Station

JUDGE HENRY J. FRIENDLY of the United States Court of Appeals for the Second Circuit has referred to "the Bill of Rights as a code of criminal procedure." In actuality, it is the entire federal Constitution that serves as a framework for the legal relationship between the policeman and the civilian, not simply the first ten Amendments, which constitute the Bill of Rights.

In essence, the problem of criminal procedure springs from the conflict in a democracy between majority rule (the community) and the rights of the minority (the accused person). The reconciliation of these often competing interests is not easy to achieve. On one hand, criminal procedure has the objectives of protecting life and property and of maintaining public peace. On the other hand, as in totalitarian countries, the agencies of law enforcement may serve as instruments of oppression, destroying innocent people and, ultimately, ending freedom for all. Historically, the United States Constitution was the culmination of a struggle against the latter type of oppression. It is important to examine some of its provisions.

CONSTITUTION OF THE UNITED STATES
AMENDMENTS IV, V, VI, VIII, XIV

AMENDMENT IV. The right of the people to be secure in their persons, houses, papers, and effects, against unreasonable searches and seizures, shall not be violated, and no Warrants shall issue, but upon probable cause, supported by oath or affirmation, and particularly describing the place to be searched, and the persons or things to be seized.

AMENDMENT V. No person shall be held to answer for a capital, or otherwise infamous crime, unless on a presentment or indictment of a Grand Jury, except in cases arising in the land or naval forces, or in the Militia, when in actual service in time of War or public danger; nor shall any person be subject for the same offence to be twice put in jeopardy of life or limb, nor shall be compelled in any criminal case to be a witness against himself, nor be deprived of life, liberty, or property, without due process of law; nor shall private property be taken for public use, without just compensation.

AMENDMENT VI. In all criminal prosecutions, the accused shall enjoy the right to a speedy and public trial, by an impartial jury of the State and district wherein the crime shall have been committed, which district shall have been previously ascertained by law, and to be informed of the nature and cause of the accusation; to be confronted with the witnesses against him; to have compulsory process for obtaining Witnesses in his favor, and to have the Assistance of Counsel for his defence.

AMENDMENT VIII. Excessive bail shall not be required, nor excessive fines imposed, nor cruel and unusual punishments inflicted.

AMENDMENT XIV. Section 1. All persons born or naturalized in the United States, and subject to the jurisdiction thereof, are citizens of the United States and of the State wherein they reside. No State shall make or enforce any law which shall abridge the privileges or immunities of citizens of the United States; nor shall any State deprive any person of life, liberty, or property, without due process of law; nor deny to any person within its jurisdiction the equal protection of the laws.

[Sections 2, 3, and 4 are omitted.]

Section 5. The Congress shall have power to enforce, by appropriate legislation, the provisions of this article.

HISTORIC DEVELOPMENT OF CONSTITUTIONAL GUARANTEES

Before the American Revolution, the individual colony had virtually exclusive control of criminal procedures within its own territory. However, the fundamental laws of England and the right of appeal to the Privy Council of the Crown did serve as some minimal check on arbitrary action.

For a period of about a hundred years after the Revolution, there was no national restriction on local criminal procedures as had existed before the break from England. Each state was supreme in matters of criminal administration. The United States Constitution only forbade the states from passing laws that designated a past act by an individual a crime, if the act was not criminal when committed (ex post facto laws). The so-called Bill of Rights (the first ten amendments to the Constitution) did not restrict the law enforcement agencies of the state: they were directed against federal law enforce ment agencies alone.

This state of affairs continued until 1866, when the Fourteen Amendment was added to the United States Constitution. The Amendment ultimately served to impose many of the requirement of the Bill of Rights on state criminal procedure, in addition to other obligations. The Fourteenth Amendment required that "no state shall deprive any person of life, liberty or property without due process of law, nor deny to any person within its jurisdiction, the equal protection of the laws."

The key phrases are "equal protection of the laws" and "due process of law." The idea of "due process of law" had been well established in the law before the adoption of the Fourteenth Amendment It had been used in English law as early as the fourteenth century That great fountainhead of individual rights, the Magna Charta recited the phrase "law of the land" in the thirteenth century. Both "due process of law"' and "law of the land" seem to have been employed to express the same idea in English law. They subsequently showed up in colonial documents and in colonial laws. In 1789, when the Constitution of the United States was originally drafted, neither expression was used in its text. But when the Bill of Rights was added the Fifth Amendment, in part, provided that the federal government could not act without "due process of law." It did not impose the requirement on the individual states that they act only by "due process of law."

Most of the constitutions that the states had adopted during the Revolution contained the same limitation on action by the state, but they used the language, "law of the land" rather than "due process of law." Virtually all the state constitutions which were adopted in the years that followed 1789 contained the same idea, but used the language "due process of law." Therefore, when in 1866 the Fourteenth Amendment was incorporated into the federal Constitution providing that "no state shall deprive any person of life, liberty, or property without due process of law," it was simply repeating a requirement that the various states had imposed upon themselves in their own constitutions. Apparently it was repeated in the United States Constitution as a restriction on the states, because it was feared that the states might not comply with the "due process of law," called for by their own constitutions, so far as the newly freed Negros were concerned. For that reason, it was re-emphasized in the federal Constitution. The incorporation in the Fourteenth Amendment of the rule that the states use "due process of law" in all their actions did not arouse much interest, because it was not anything new.

The inclusion of the due process of law requirement in the Fourteenth Amendment of the federal Constitution, seemingly innocuous, ultimately became the cornerstone for the supervisory role taken on by the Supreme Court of the United States and the federal courts over all acts of the state governments. It was a catalyst for an unforeseen new relationship between the national and state governments. In the last two decades, it has become apparent that the Fourteenth Amendment has served as the instrument for bringing about revolutionary changes in the administration of criminal justice.

The role of the Supreme Court in setting standards of criminal procedure to which the state courts had to conform was not realized at first. In 1880, the Supreme Court was urged to reverse a criminal conviction by a state court on the ground that there were different appellate courts in various areas of the state and that such failure to maintain a uniform system of appeals by the state deprived the defendant of his right to "due process of law" under the Fourteenth Amendment. The Supreme Court refused to honor this argument. It also refused to honor similar arguments seeking to apply the due process clause of the Fourteenth Amendment to state criminal procedures.

In the next fifty years, such questions were raised in a growing number of cases. The first state criminal case was reversed in 1927 on this ground, when the Supreme Court decided that a trial by a justice of the peace, who received a fee if he convicted the defendant but none if the defendant was cleared, constituted a denial of due process of law. The volume of criminal convictions appealed to the Supreme Court of the United States has steadily increased for half a century and in the last decade has risen to torrential proportions. A goodly number of convictions have been reversed by the highest court of the land on the ground that due process of law has been denied.

In subsequent discussions of various aspects of criminal procedure, detailed examination will be made of requirements of due process as applied to specific situations. It is noteworthy that, time after time, the Supreme Court has said that the Fourteenth Amendment does not automatically require the states to use all criminal procedure that the United States Constitution requires in federal criminal cases. For instance, it does not make it mandatory that indictment be only by grand jury, or that all criminal trials be conducted by jury.

The Supreme Court has said that the administration of criminal justice by the states shall be such as to afford the accused a "principle of justice so rooted in the traditions and conscience of our people as to be ranked as fundamental." And these procedures "shall be consistent with the fundamental principles of liberty and justice which lie at the base of our civil and political institutions."

As a result of this federal-state constitutional system, the pattern of state criminal procedures must comply with the requirements of the individual state constitution. And there is not much difference among the states in many matters. In addition, there is the superior requirement imposed on the state criminal procedures by the Fourteenth Amendment to the United States Constitution, that of "due process of law" as applied from time to time in the cases decided by the Supreme Court.

In addition to the due process clause in the Fourteenth Amendment that enables federal courts to supervise standards of criminal procedure, the same Amendment specifically empowers Congress to "enforce by appropriate legislation the provisions of [the Fourteenth] Amendment." It is hard to believe, but Congress has not enacted any laws specifically prescribing appropriate state court procedure, except for a statute passed in 1875 which forbade discrimination on the basis of race in the selection of members of juries.

Almost a hundred years ago, Congress passed a statute pursuant to the Fourteenth Amendment, which has been dormant until recently. As enacted in 1870, it punishes any person who, "under color of any law, statute, ordinance, regulation or custom willfully subjects [another] to the deprivation of any rights, privileges or immunities secured or protected by the Constitution or law of the United States." This act has been invoked more and more frequently against local police officers, who have been charged with going beyond their authority in connection with making arrests, detaining persons, or coercing confessions.

The Supreme Court of the United States has, in a long line of conflicting cases, shown that it cannot resolve differences in interpretation and application of this statute by the Judges of the Court. Yet Congress has not seen fit to pass legislation that would work out the differences or clarify the law. It is patent that a good deal of the confusion and furor surrounding procedures to be applied in the state administration of criminal justice would be obviated by federal legislation enacted in furtherance of the objectives of the Fourteenth Amendment.

To this point, the discussion has concerned itself chiefly with the federal supervision of state criminal procedures resulting from the Fourteenth Amendment to the federal Constitution. The role of the federal Constitution in supervising federal criminal procedures is much more clear. The Constitution as originally adopted contained the guarantee of a jury trial. The Bill of Rights, which became efective on December 15, 1791, through its Fourth, Fifth, Sixth, and Eighth Amendments, prohibited unreasonable searches and seizures, compulsory self-incrimination, and excessive bail. It required grand jury indictment, confrontation of witnesses, assistance of counsel, information of the nature and cause of the accusation, and of course, due process of law. The Supreme Court of the United States has spelled out the scope and application of these guarantees in federal criminal cases coming on appeal before it. In addition, for about a decade, the Supreme Court has used the rule-making power delegated to it by Congress to establish rules for the administration of criminal proceedings in the federal courts.

JUSTICE IN THE "GATEHOUSE"

An important and interesting development in the field of constitutional law as applied to the administration of criminal justice has been the increasing concern with the procedures employed in the police station rather than with those used in the courtroom.

Arguments for Extension of Rights

Professor Yale Kamisar, of the University of Michigan Law School, has compared conditions in the "gatehouse" (the police station) with those in the "mansion" (the courtroom) as part of the routine administration of criminal law.[1]

He writes that, in the "gatehouse," "the enemy of the state is a depersonalized subject to be sized up and subjected to interrogation tactics and techniques . . . appropriate for the occasion. He is game to be stalked."

In sharp comparison, writes Kamisar, "once he leaves the 'gatehouse' and enters the 'mansion'—if he ever gets there (most defendants plead guilty and don't)—the enemy of the state is repersonalized, even dignified, the public invited and a strong ceremony in honor of individual freedom from law enforcement celebrated."

Kamisar contends that the conflict between the individual and the state is mediated by an impartial judge in the courtroom, but that, in the police station, "although the same conflict exists in more aggravated form, the law passes it by.

"In the courtroom the defendant is presumed innocent; in the police station the proceedings usually begin, 'All right—we know you're guilty; come through and it'll be easier for you.'"

The lawyer never leaves the side of the defendant in the courtroom, yet, in the police station, the suspect might not have his lawyer with him, even if he were advised of his rights to retain counsel. The defendant in the "mansion" not only is not required to answer questions, unless he decides to take the stand, he cannot be asked for an explanation of why he chooses to remain silent. In the "gatehouse," "even if the suspect is that rare and troublesome type who knows of (he is not likely to be told) and insists on his right to remain silent, his interrogators simply will not let him."

Professor Kamisar claims that "police interrogators may now hurl jolting questions where once they swung telephone books, may now play on the emotions where once they resorted to physical violence. But it is no less true today than it was thirty years ago that, quoting Ernest J. Hopkins, 'in every city our police hold what can only be called outlaw tribunals—informal and secret inquisitions of arrested persons—which are, terminology aside, actual and very vigorous trials of crime. Centering all upon the confession, proud of it, staking everything upon it, the major canon of American police work is based upon the nullification of the most truly libertarian abuse of the Fifth Amendment.' "

Law enforcement officials and members of the Bench and Bar who have accepted the many procedural rights that envelop the accused in the "mansion" are bitterly fighting the extension of those rights to the "gatehouse." The philosophy of this position is forcefully expressed in the words of Harold Gray, the originator of the comic strip, "Little Orphan Annie," using his heroine as his oracle. On September 24, 1965, in his syndicated strip he depicted a brave "lawman" who complains as follows:

> Oh, I suppose a unlettered hillbilly like me cain't be expected to git a'holt o' th' finer points o' this new sweetness and light gruel they're preachin': . . . But ah was brung up t' believe th' law was to protect th' law-abidin' and honest folks! When any feller went outside th' law, he chanced gettin' kilt! 'Course, if he got caught alive he had a right to a fair trial!
> But what biles me is how come all t'oncet dirty murderers git *all* th' protection and th' victims don't even git their names spelt right in their death notices?

The police chief commiserates with him:

> Yep! Tryin' to be a good cop can be a discouraging business, in lots of places!

Others have voiced the same plaint, perhaps more eloquently and grammatically, but not more effectively. The police chief of Los Angeles, William H. Parker, has expressed the view that the job of the policeman in America has been "tragically weakened" by the enroaching "judicial takeover." The past president of the National Association of District Attorneys, Garrett Byrne, who is now a member of the President's National Crime Commission, has expressed the idea even more strongly, stating that the Supreme Court is "destroying the nation."

Certain commentators have voiced the idea that the recent decisions of the Supreme Court relating to criminal procedure do not cause crime, but rather that crime is caused by many other complex factors in society. A Deputy Attorney-General of the United States has expressed the view:

> People do not commit crime because they know they cannot be questioned by police before presentment, or even because they feel they will not be convicted.

Professor Herbert Wechsler of Columbia Law School, who is a director of the American Law Institute and a draftsman of the Model Penal Code, said some time ago, in *"A Caveat on Crime Control"*:

> The most satisfactory method of crime prevention is the solution of the basic problems of government—the production and distribution of external goods, education and recreation. . . . That the problems of social reform present dilemmas of their own, I do not pretend to deny. I argue only that one can say for social reform as a means to the end of improved crime control what can also be said for better personnel but cannot be said for drastic tightening of the processes of the criminal law—that even if the end should not be achieved, the means is desirable for its own sake.[2]

And Dean Erwin Griswold of the Harvard Law School, in an address delivered on August 9, 1965, entitled "The Long View," has taken a position in support of the direction the Supreme Court enunciated in the field of criminal procedure:

> Is it not clear, in the long view of history, that the time has come for us to bring ourselves up to a new level in the administration of criminal justice in this country, and that the Supreme Court is obeying not only the mandate of the Constitution but also the natural progress of history in taking steps to bring us to a higher level? The process may be painful in individual cases. There is an understandable reluctance to have to adjust to new standards. But the process can be better understood, and more readily accepted, when it is more widely recognized that the concern of the Supreme Court has been primarily directed toward the long view, toward long-range goals and ideals embodied in the Constitution, while the natural and understandable concern of its critics has more often been focused on short-range application of old principles, and upon more immediate concerns.

One is struck by a statement uttered by a Judge of the Supreme Court of South Africa, who, after investigating American judicial and police institutions and procedures, concluded that our law-enforcement officers give only token obeisance to the constitutional requirements. In fact, he took the position that they did not meet standards adhered to by South African police officers:

> As a Judge of the Supreme Court of South Africa recently observed, despite a great deal of emotional writing which elevates the privilege against self-incrimination to "one of the great landmarks in man's struggle to make himself civilized", the most abundant proof that it does not prohibit pretrial interrogation is to be found in the United States.
>
> There the privilege is in the federal Constitution and in some form or other in the constitutions of all but two of the fifty states. . . . But in none of the forty-nine jurisdictions does it apply to what happens in the police station. The police interrogate freely, sometimes for seven to eight hours on end. The statements thus extracted are given in evidence. There is the provision that only statements made voluntarily may be given in evidence, *but that seems to be interpreted rather liberally, judged by our standards!* [Italics supplied.]

And consider the statement of former Senator (now Judge) Keating in his speech to the Harvard Legal Aid Bureau Annual Banquet in 1965, when he said as follows:

> I think it is probably fair to say the indigent persons generally, but especially those who are alleged to be not among the law-abiding, are at the tender mercies of all the rest of us, especially those who sit in the Halls of Congress. We are all aware of the weighty influence wielded, for example, by the organized medical profession and the organized bar upon legislation in Congress. It has become commonplace to speak to the "A.M.A. lobby" or, in the education field, the "N.E.A. lobby." But there is no lobby of the A.C.D.A. The American Criminal Defendants' Association. . . .
>
> Fortunately, there are groups such as the American Civil Liberties Union and the NAACP, which take a strong interest in the administration of the criminal law as it affects the disadvantaged defendant. But their voice in the legislative process is diluted by the fact that the clientele group for which they purport to speak normally exercises little political power, and, in fact, those in the group who have been convicted of felony have been by law politically sterilized. . . .
>
> This is the key explanation of why the recognition of the rights of indigents has been largely confined to the judicial process. And it is one of the great ironies of American life, and always has been, that the Congress and State legislatures will be critical of judicial lawmaking particularly in the administration of criminal justice, while failing to recognize that the courts cannot but respond firmly to social necessity when the legislative branch abdicates responsibilities for constructive action.

Arguments Against Extension of Rights

It cannot be denied that the average policeman has a difficult job, one which is becoming even more difficult. He must cope with the restrictions imposed by the judges on "Mt. Olympus," and he feels that he is handcuffed in doing his job. Prof. Fred E. Inbau waxes indignant about the "professional" civil libertarian:

> One reason why the law would remain unchanged is the concern that would be voiced by various persons and by various civil liberty groups against allowing any encroachment upon the right to be let alone. Consider, for instance, the incident in Los Angeles a few years ago, involving the thirty-year-old son of a famous judge with an ultra civil libertarian viewpoint. He was walking along a street at night in a neighborhood in which there had been a number of recent burglaries. A policeman in a patrol car stopped to inquire who he was. He refused to identify himself. He wanted to test his civil rights.

He argues that the citizen is protected when the police officer is conscientious, well trained, and free from "political interference."

> The FBI has made effective use of wiretapping in its investigations, but very little is ever heard of this activity because the information so obtained is used only as a lead and is not itself offered as evidence in court. And despite the fact that the FBI conducts its wiretap operations without court permission or supervision, it has not been accused of misusing its wiretap facilities and operations for other than laudable purposes—a fact which signals the following truism about law enforcement and the preservation of civil liberties and personal privacy: the only real assurance an individual, law-abiding citizen has against the misuse of police power is to see that our police forces—national, state and local—are selected and promoted on a merit basis, properly trained, adequately compensated, internally supervised against abusive practices, and permitted to remain free from politically inspired interference. With police forces of this caliber there will be a minimum degree of abusive practices. This freedom from abuse cannot be achieved by artificial and unwarranted restrictions upon necessary police functions.

Professor Inbau with one sentence sums up his position.

> Nor is it the constitutional function of the courts to police the police.[3]

The Constitution is now in the police station. It is not likely that it will be leaving soon.

V.

Requirements of a Valid Arrest

Arrest on Suspicion

THE WHEELS of the machinery of criminal procedure usually begin to turn when the police officer makes his first move. That move is frequently the arrest. While the idea of an arrest seems simple, it involves complicated legal issues. Often the arrest is challenged in court because the policeman forgot to observe one of the legal requirements in his zeal to enforce the law.

An illegal arrest is a violation of law and of individual rights. Its most frequent occurrence is in the arrest "on suspicion" or "for investigation"—that is, when there is no concrete evidence that a definite crime has been committed. Yet the law is clear. No arrest can be made without a warrant, based simply on nebulous suspicions. The policeman must have "probable cause" to believe that the person held has perpetrated a definite crime. The extent of arrests for no specific crime may be estimated when it showed that in 1960, local police departments reported 136,325 arrests on suspicion to the FBI.

At times, such arrests are conducted by swarms of police officers who swoop down on a neighborhood where many crimes have been taking place (almost invariably poverty-stricken and inhabited by racial minorities) and gather hordes of people without "probable cause." Thus, following a number of attacks on women in Detroit in 1960 and 1961, and immediately after the homicide of Mrs. Betty James, Commissioner Ward commanded the return to "old-fashioned methods of police patrol," and as many as one thousand people were stopped on the streets, searched, and arrested. The large majority of these persons was not guilty of any crime. Yet, the Police Commissioner explained that, "This is a desperate situation requiring desperate measures." [1] There are other illustrations. In a study made in the District of Columbia, it was determined that seventeen out of each eighteen persons arrested between 1960 and 1961 were not charged with a specific crime. The principal recommendation of the study was clear: "The cost to the community is more than the practice is worth. Legally, the practice cannot be justified. The practice should stop, and stop immediately." [2]

Definition of Arrest

Under the criminal law, an arrest amounts to taking a person into custody, under actual or assumed authority, either to compel him to answer a criminal charge or to prevent him from committing a criminal act. Whether an arrest has actually taken place may present a difficult factual and legal problem. Accosting a person, and nothing more, does not constitute an arrest. The American Law Institute, in its Model Code of Criminal Procedure, has defined arrest as "the taking of a person into custody that he may be forthcoming to answer for the commission of any offense."[3] Although there is no magic ritual or formula that must be adhered to, certain requirements must be met. They have been stated this way:

"To constitute an arrest there must be an intent to arrest under a real or pretended authority, accompanied by a seizure or detention of the person which is so understood by the person arrested."[4]

Usually, the requirement of detention contemplates a physical seizure of the person who is arrested. But this is not absolutely essential. There are situations in which a mere touching of the person will be sufficient to constitute a legal arrest. And under some circumstances, a mere statement by the police officer, asserting an arrest, followed by acquiescence by the person to whom the words are spoken, will be considered an arrest in the eyes of the law. This is so even though force has not been used and the person arrested has not even been touched. In order for the arrest to have been made technically, the policeman must intend to hold the person in order to take the initial steps of criminal prosecution such as fingerprinting, booking, and arraigning. Since the intention of the arresting officer cannot be actually ascertained, reliance must be placed on what he said and did to learn his intention.

Generally, any person who is considered capable of being charged with a crime may be arrested. However, there are some constitutional and statutory provisions that protect such persons as Congressmen, members of state legislature, and foreign diplomats, in varying degrees.

Arrest With a Warrant

A warrant is a document signed by a judge, which authorizes a policeman, or other appropriate peace officer, to make an arrest.

Justices of the peace were first established in 1326. At first, they were empowered to arrest. Gradually, they acquired authority to direct the constable to make the arrest. They issued warrants to several people to make an arrest if a search had to be made for the suspect. By 1848, the right to issue warrants was expressly recognized by statute.

ARREST WITH A WARRANT IN THE UNITED STATES

The two essential requisites of a valid warrant are that the court which issues the warrant must have legal power to do so, and the warrant must not have any defect that appears on its face which is so serious that it voids the issuance. It is not often that warrants are invalid on either ground, because, generally, a court operates within its jurisdiction and the warrant forms are fairly standardized. Most arrests at the present time are made without a warrant. These are the arrests that most often cause questions to be posed.

Before a warrant will be issued, a complaint is made, under oath or affirmation, alleging that a crime has been perpetrated and that there is "probable cause" to suspect the person named. These prerequisites are required by the federal and state constitutions. And it is also usually required that the facts that constitute the basis for probable cause are within the personal knowledge and belief of the person making the complaint rather than merely suspicions based on information derived from others. A policeman, or other peace officer, as a matter of ordinary practice, holds the warrant until he is able to arrest the person described. Frequently, there is no record kept of the issuance of the warrant—or even that the warrant was executed or not executed.

Validity of the Warrant

A warrant may seem valid, yet be invalid. The court issuing the warrant might not enjoy the authority to issue a warrant covering the offense for which it was issued. Or the court issuing the warrant might not have jurisdiction over the person named or over the territory where the warrant is to be used. If the court only has the legal authority to issue warrants for specific offenses, the policeman is supposed to be aware of the restricted scope of the court's authority and may not make an arrest for any other crime. Or the statute may require that prosecution for a certain offense is to be commenced by a *summons*. A warrant that has been issued to arrest a person for that certain offense is invalid.

The validity of the warrant does not depend upon whether the person arrested is in fact guilty. But the warrant is invalid if the person to be arrested is not accurately named or, at least, accurately described. If there are a number of persons with the same name, the arrest of the wrong person can be set aside. However, if the arrested person uses two names and one of them is recited in the warrant, the arrest will be upheld.

In some situations, the name of the person to be arrested is not known. The warrant is sufficient if it so states and then sets forth a description sufficient to describe the person.

Arrest Without a Warrant

A deep-seated tradition in the American legal system is its repugnance toward arbitrary arrest. This is expressed in Article IV of the Constitution of the United States, and every state constitution contains similar provisions. However, these constitutional provisions have not been deemed to prohibit arrests without warrants. The courts have held that the constitutional requirement is violated only if a warrant is issued without a proper legal basis. It has been acknowledged by the courts that the legislatures under the state police power can pass laws authorizing arrests even without warrants, provided that the statutes enacted do not violate the constitutional requirements of due process of law or those rights reserved to the people.

At the present time, most states have rules relating to arrests without a warrant incorporated into legislation. Before the passage of such statutes, usually, a policeman or other peace officer or even a private citizen had each almost the same legal right to arrest without a warrant. Any one of them could arrest without a warrant to prevent or stop acts of treason, felonies, or breaches of the peace. After a breach of the peace was committed, an arrest without a warrant could be made only if the act had been committed in the presence of the person making the arrest, and only if followed by immediate and continued pursuit. If a felony or treason had really been committed, and if "reasonable grounds" for suspecting the defendant existed, he could be arrested without a warrant. If, in actuality, no treason or felony had been committed, but the policeman had reasonable grounds to believe that the suspect had committed one, he could arrest without a warrant. A private citizen did not have the same right to make an arrest without a warrant. And, in absence of statute, there could not be an arrest made without a warrant for any misdemeanor but a breach of peace.

The common-law rights of private persons to make arrests without a warrant have been modified by statute. Thus, in a few states, a private citizen may make an arrest without a warrant where any misdemeanor, not just a breach of peace, is committed in his presence. Usually, while arrest for misdemeanor could be made by private person without a warrant at common law, this right has not been continued by most statutes.

There are not many statutory provisions that expand the common-law rules covering the right of a private citizen to arrest for a felony without a warrant. The private person is still restricted to make an arrest for a felony actually committed to when he has reasonable grounds to suspect the guilt of the arrested person, or to prevent a crime from being committed, or where a felony has actually been committed in his presence.

The trend in legislation is to increase the right of the policeman to make arrests. By many statutes, the policeman may make an arrest without a warrant for any misdemeanor committed in his presence, in addition to his authority in felonies to make such arrests. The officer may arrest a person who has actually committed a felony, even though the crime was not committed in his presence and regardless of whether he completely believes the arrested person committed it. Under statutory law, as at common law, if a felony has been committed and the officer has reasonable grounds to believe that the person arrested committed it, an arrest may be made without a warrant. Likewise, an arrest can be made without a warrant by a policeman if he has reasonable grounds to believe that a felony is being or has been committed and to believe that the person arrested is the one who is committing or has committed it. About one third of the states have adopted this rule.

In the absence of authorization by statute, the policeman has only his common-law right to arrest without a warrant, and only for a misdemeanor that is considered a breach of the peace. The rationale for such a rule is that, where there is a breach of peace, there is no time to go to court for a warrant, and, also, intervention by a policeman can prevent serious injury or property damage. Where there is such a breach of peace, the policeman may arrest all those who seem to be participating in the fracas, as well as those who are actually involved. There is no legal requirement—as there is when a private citizen is making the arrest—that the policeman actually witness the arrested person participating in the disturbance.

In Kansas, Missouri, New Jersey, Pennsylvania, Virginia, and Washington, the courts by their decisions have indicated that there may be arrests made by policemen, without warrants, for any misdemeanors committed in their presence. The federal courts have taken a similar view with respect to arrests by federal law-enforcement agents, even where the acts do not amount to a breach of peace. A number of states have statutes with this provision.

Manner of Making an Arrest

The basic rule about the time of a valid arrest is that it may be made at any time of the day, any day of the week. Some statutes prohibit arrest on Sundays or at night, except in certain situations. The validity of an arrest is decided on the basis of the law in the place where the arrest is made. Usually, an arrest in one state cannot be made for an alleged violation of a law in another state, unless there is reciprocal legislation between the states involved. Under the federal Constitution, various treaties between the United States and other countries, and compacts among a number of states, provide for the arrest and extradition of fugitives.

Unless there is some special authorization by statute a policeman or other peace officer cannot make an arrest outside the jurisdiction where he received his appointment and was authorized to act.

Possession of a Warrant

If, at the time of making the arrest, the policeman did not have the warrant in his possession, the legal effect will be the same as if there was no warrant in existence at the time of the arrest. The decision will not be affected by the fact that the person arrested did not demand to be shown the warrant or did not know that a warrant had not been issued. If a warrant is not in the possession of the policeman, and if a warrant is legally required under the circumstances to make an arrest, the person arrested may resist the arrest. The policeman may be held for assault if he persists in effecting the arrest by force in this situation. These rules are also operative in cases where a policeman gets someone to help him make an arrest under these circumstances.

Use of Force in Making an Arrest

A police officer who is engaged in making a valid arrest may use any amount of force that may be necessary to restrain the person arrested and to protect himself. However, he is not entitled to use *more* than the force than is required, within reason. The person who claims that an unreasonable amount of force was employed has the burden of proof establishing that contention. If the policeman asks a civilian to help him in making an arrest, that person has the same legal protection as the policeman. However, where the attempted arrest is not proper, the police officer is acting wrongfully and may be resisted in self-defense. Apparently, the degree of force that will be sanctioned in arresting a person for a felony is greater than in the case of a misdemeanor. In a felony, under some circumstances, the courts will sanction taking the life of the person who is resisting. But, in arresting a person for a misdemeanor, the policeman is usually not authorized to harm physically or imperil the life of the person arrested. In any case, the policeman may if necessary kill a person resisting arrest if it is necessary to protect the officer's own life.

Entry to Make an Arrest

When the policeman has a warrant, he may break down the door to a house or an apartment to arrest a person inside, as a general rule. This is also true when the policeman is entitled to make an arrest without a warrant. However, in general, neither a policeman nor a private person may break into an abode, with or without a warrant, in order to arrest anyone, until he has first informed those within of the reason for his entry and has been refused entrance.

Obligations of Civilians to Help

The policeman may call on a passerby to help him in carrying out his duty in making an arrest. Such a civilian is invested with the same authority as the policeman who called upon him. A civilian who has not been requested to help, but who volunteers in making an arrest, does so at his own peril. If a citizen refuses to aid an officer, when called upon to do so, he may be indicted himself.

Treatment of the Arrested Person

The policeman who has made an arrest has the obligation to treat the person arrested in a proper way, according to law. He can hold him in jail for only a limited period before bringing him before the court that issued the warrant. He can question him in the proper place designated for that purpose, but he cannot subject him to coercion or duress. The prisoner's right to counsel will be discussed later on. The policeman does not have the right to place handcuffs on the prisoner unless this is actually necessary to prevent his escape. The police may photograph and fingerprint the prisoner. And, as part of a valid arrest, the police may search the prisoner and take from him any property that may aid him to escape or may incriminate him. If property is taken from a prisoner after his arrest, he continues to have a claim on it, and it will ultimately be returned to him. If it is connected with the alleged crime, the trial court will make an order regarding its disposition.

Remedies for Illegal Arrest

The person who has been the victim of an illegal arrest may choose among a number of alternative remedies. He may bring suit for money damages against the police officer, the policeman's supervisors, or the governmental unit itself, whether city, state, or federal government. Not very many lawsuits for damages are brought against the policeman himself, because most policemen do not have the financial assets to make such action worthwhile. An additional factor that militates against such lawsuit is that, in many states, the wages of policemen are not subject to garnishment.

The courts will not grant an injunction to restrain a threatened illegal arrest. One reason for this is that an essential prerequisite to granting such an injunction is the threat of irresponsible loss to property or the lack of another legal remedy. Other possible means of relief are habeas corpus, in certain cases of illegal arrest, or detention in custody. In addition, the injured person may have resort to various civilian review boards, which have been created in different states.

The Anglo-American legal system does not provide automatic public compensation to innocent persons who have been illegally arrested.

VI. The Use of Force

. . . We know now that the phrase "police brutality" is not rooted in myth. It is with us in fact—and in the bitter memories and ugly scars of its victims. Once again, we are in debt to television, the true chronicler of our times.

To my mind, police brutality henceforth will mean the lunge of a uniformed cop toward a Brooklyn College girl, preparatory to dragging her off BY THE HAIR OF HER HEAD.

Police brutality is the laying about with billy clubs as students march quietly for peace. It is the wanton use of a nerve gas that causes temporary blindness. It is the kicks administered to the unarmed as they lie on the sidewalk, pushed there by the righteous arm of the law.

THESE STRONG SENTIMENTS were expressed by Harriet Van Horne in her New York *Post* column of October 20, 1967. Such charges of police brutality and the countercharges volleyed back by law enforcers are becoming louder, more strident, and more bitter every day.

The generally approved statement of law covering the use of force by a police officer is contained in the Uniform Arrest Act.[1] It is that a peace officer should not use unnecessary force in making an arrest, nor should he desist because of threatened resistance. Some states require a peace officer to make every reasonable effort to advise the person he is attempting to arrest that he is an officer, if that is not apparent. Most states permit the use of force sufficient to kill the suspect in making an arrest for any felony. Some argue that the use of deadly force should be permitted even in the case of misdemeanors, because obedience to known policeman is essential to the maintenance of public order and safety. Others would have the officer use such force only in the cases of arrests for felonies that have been perpetrated with violence.

Permissible Force—The Social Component

It is easier to state a rule than to apply it. The policeman is entitled to use that amount of force necessary to apprehend the alleged criminal. The force may consist of a push into a police car, a twist of the arm to compel the suspect to walk quietly down the street with the policeman, or a shot that kills a fleeing mugger. While the officer may increase the force he uses in proportion to the nature of the resistance, what policeman can exactly evaluate the precise amount and type of force that will cause the person to submit?

The limit on the type of force that may be resorted to by law-enforcement agents is to a large extent determined by society, at a given place and time. More than a hundred years ago, in New York City, the scourge of mid-Manhattan was a band of muggers known as the Honeymooners, who preyed on passers-by who appeared to be in comfortable financial circumstances. In 1853, Capt. George

W. Walling selected six of his brawniest police officers, decked them out in plain clothes, and distributed wooden clubs. He catapulted this "strong-arm squad" into the terrified neighborhood. They acted in a direct and simple manner. When one of the squad saw a member of the Honeymooners, he simply accosted him and flogged him unmercifully. The Honeymoon boys soon emigrated further downtown, to the Bowery and Five Points.

But social attitudes change. It would be hard to imagine, today, a public official behaving like New York's Mayor La Guardia or Police Commissioner Lewis Valentine, just twenty years ago, when inspecting a police line-up. Irritated at one of the prisoners, the Police Commissioner yelled: "He's the best-dressed man in the room. Don't be afraid to muss him up! Blood should be smeared all over that velvet collar." Mayor La Guardia encouraged him from the sidelines: "That's the way I like to hear you talk, Lew. Muss 'em up if necessary."

At about that time, a representative of the Legal Aid Society stated that, of the 8,300 persons represented by the Society in the Felony Court, almost 33 per cent showed some indication of physical injury of various types, including broken bones. Newspaper crusades and succeeding police commissioners in New York have changed this picture considerably.[2]

The common type of complaint involving the use of force by the police is illustrated by the case of Kenneth Spencer, a native of Jamaica, New York, who is attending the University of Washington as a graduate student. He recently testified before a City Council hearing in Seattle on police procedures. His statement under oath was that two policeman stopped him at night when he was returning home. They insisted that he was required to carry an identification card. He maintained that he was not required to carry one. The officers became impatient, and, according to Spencer's version, one of them said: "You smart ———, I'm going to teach you a lesson." He then allegedly proceeded to strike Spencer on the jaw and body.

Spencer then testified that the second policeman "moved in behind me, grabbed hold of my neck and began to choke me violently." He was knocked to the ground. There, the policeman put handcuffs on him. "While still lying on the ground, I was kicked." Spencer claims another beating in the police car with a flashlight, later that night. He was subsequently booked for "being abroad."

The attorney for the Seattle branch of the American Civil Liberties Union testified at the City Council that cases involving excessive force or brutality by the police frequently concern petty or minor offenses. They rarely come to the attention of district attorneys, judges, juries, or lawyers. Said their counsel, Alvin Ziontz, "Apparently, any so-called back-talk from a prisoner triggers violence. The most inflammatory statement a prisoner can make to a Seattle policeman is, 'I know my constitutional rights'."

It may be observed that the victims of excessive force or physical abuse at the hands of the police are usually members of minority groups, marginal people—those who would be afraid to complain. Two incidents will illustrate this observation.

Mary Brown [fictitious name], a Negro prostitute, was together with a white married male companion in a Detroit house. A police officer sought admittance and, when he came in, his presence threw the customer into a panic. In his consternation, the man complained that Mary had stolen three dollars from him. This made Mary Brown furious, and she exclaimed: "I wouldn't make the joint hot for three measly bucks."

She continued her tirade, now directed against the police, and her protestations of innocence in the patrol car on the way to the police station. One of the policeman warned her: "If you don't shut up, I'm going to put you in the hospital." In spite of the fact that she was in handcuffs, Mary was still belligerent. When they arrived at the police station, Mary kicked out, but claimed that she did not hit anyone. The police hurled her to the ground. One of them jerked her up off the floor and bashed her face against the wall. When the police booked her, Mary was adamant about making her own accusation. When she was finally taken to the hospital, the entry on the hospital admission record stated: "Injured herself while falling out of patrol car."

Mary continued to assert herself. She sought the assistance of the N.A.A.C.P. The law officers took her into custody once more and sought to induce her to swear that it was her pimp who had given her a going-over. The man who ran the bar from which she operated was warned: "She's hot, keep her out." Even the customer, in whose company she had been first picked up, gave an affidavit that Mary had been hurt by falling from a police car. However, Mary Brown refused to withdraw her complaint. Other witnesses were located. Finally, the Civil Rights Commission decided in her favor, and the policemen involved were shifted to different assignments.

Another case is that of Theodore Jones. On a hot Saturday night, July 24, 1965, Teddy, twenty years old, and his girl friend, Anne Lucas, went to Coney Island with a group of other young people. After enjoying the rides, they joined about 150 youngsters who were dancing to recorded music being played outside the Himalaya ride.

It was after midnight, and a passing policeman apparently advised the teen-agers that they could continue dancing for five minutes more.

A few minutes later, another policeman, Arthur Crichlow, a Negro in his twenties, directed the youngsters dancing to stop. Teddy complained in a loud voice, "One cop tells you one thing, one cop tells you another." An argument ensued, and finally police officer Crichlow said to Teddy, "OK. I'm taking you in."

The patrolman asked for identification, and the young man gave him his wallet. Anne Lucas related, "The cop just stands there looking at the wallet for about five minutes, and Teddy gets tired of waiting, so he reaches for the wallet, and the cop pulls the wallet back and grabs Teddy by the shirt. Teddy was talking pretty loud, but he wasn't cursing or nothing, and the policeman says, Don't embarrass me in front of all these people.'

"And the next thing he does is to take the billy and hit Teddy right across the brow over his left eye."

The policeman's version is that he was examining the wallet when the young man abruptly made a grab for it. The patrolman explained that he acted "instinctively" and hit Teddy over the head with his night stick.

The youth was helped to a car and transported to the station house. From there, he was taken by ambulance to Coney Island Hospital, where he arrived at two A.M. He was X-rayed and given six stitches in his head. He was then brought back to the police station, where he remained for five hours before he was taken before a judge. The notes of the court stenographer reflect that a court officer stated that Jones "doesn't look good," and Crichlow answered, "He's drunk."

The judge put off the hearing, and, after Teddy was examined by another doctor, he was sent to Kings County Hospital on Sunday afternoon at three o'clock. There they discovered that the youth's skull was fractured: Following a four-and-a-half-hour operation, Teddy died.

The family has brought a civil suit against New York City for monetary damages. However, a grand jury has cleared the police officer. He may still face a police department administrative hearing on a complaint made by the attorney for the Jones family.

Use of Force by a Policeman Off Duty

In New York City, a policeman is considered on duty all the time. He is required to carry his gun with him except when he is asleep. As a comparison, in Boston, the police officer is not on his job once he arrives home. He takes off his weapon and his uniform. There are less off-duty incidents in Boston.

In early 1965, patrolman Edward Ryan, age twenty-nine, was relaxing in his off hours with a friend, aged twenty-five, named Thomas

McConn, in a New York City bar. McConn and another young man became embroiled in an argument. They left the bar to continue it. Ryan intervened to break up the fight. Although Ryan identified himself as a patrolman, Owens, the stranger, continued to fight and punched Ryan. At that point, Ryan drew his revolver. It went off by mistake, and Owens was killed.

Consider the case of a policeman who discovered two men urinating on a hedge when he was off duty and leaving his home. He became incensed and called them "pigs," following his words with a sock to the chin of one of them. Because of his righteous anger and reaction, he was brought up on charges and fined five days' pay.

Use of Force—Nature of the Crime

The general rule is that the officer may use such force as is necessary to arrest the suspect or to keep him in custody or to recapture him after escape. The difficulty is in defining what is meant by "necessary." The policeman is taught that he may use such force as is necessary to make an arrest, and to use his gun only if there is no other alternative. But there are many other factors to consider in deciding what is "necessary." What may not be necessary for an experienced policeman may be necessary for one who has only recently joined the police force. If the officer is a big, burly man, necessity means something different than if he is a lithe youngster.

Permissible force certainly will be defined differently if the police officer is accompanied by brother officers or civilians who can help him. And, of course, there are different considerations involved in arresting a hardened criminal, burdened by a record of violence, and arresting a person who has parked his car in a No Parking zone. It is impossible for a policeman to make the same sort of rational, objective judgments at a time of split-second crisis as a jury may make several months after the arrest—from the safety of the jury box. The police officer's action must therefore be "reasonable" action, in view of facts and circumstances as they presented themselves at the time of the incident.

FORCE IN ARRESTING FOR A FELONY

The test of reasonable force is pegged to some extent on the nature of the crime involved. It places quite a burden on the police officer that he be required to decide, before he acts, whether he is facing a felony or a misdemeanor. If there has been a killing, the police officer can be fairly sure of the amount of force he may use. But if the precise classification of the crime is questionable, the policeman must proceed at his own risk.

Is it essential that a felony must have been actually committed by the suspect, or is it sufficient if the police officer has a reasonable basis to believe that it has been? California, Georgia, Maryland, Massachusetts, North Carolina, Oklahoma, Tennessee, Virginia, Washington, and possibly Florida are states in which it is enough to arrest if the policeman has reasonable grounds for suspicion, according to common-law decisions. These states are joined by New Hampshire, Rhode Island, and South Carolina, which have adopted the same rule by statute. A minority of states holds that the police officer acts at his peril: he must be absolutely right in his evaluation. The states so holding are Kentucky, Pennsylvania, West Virginia, and possibly Arizona. They are joined by Alaska and Pennsylvania, which by statute share the same view. In Minnesota, Nevada, and New York, the rule seems to be that the felony must have been committed by someone, but not necessarily the suspect.

Thus, if the crime for which the arrest is being made is characterized as a felony, it may be lawful for the police officer to use force enough to kill the suspect in making the arrest. Also, the amount and nature of the force employed may vary with the sort of resistance offered to the arrest, whether it be fighting or flight. Different circumstances yield different results.

Force Against a Fleeing Felon

At common law, all felonies were punishable by death. Therefore, it was not strange that resistance to arrest for a felony, including flight, could be met with death-dealing force by the police officer. Although felonies are not so harshly dealt with today, the same rule usually still applies. Where a fleeing felon cannot otherwise be captured, force resulting in death may be used. However, in absence of a different statute, the law requires a reasonable need for the use of such force. The policeman must satisfy a judge or jury that he tried in good faith and with good judgment to make the arrest—that he avoided the use of lethal force until he had no other reasonable choice.

Nature of Reasonable Necessity

The factors involved in deciding whether force was reasonably necessary are complex. Among the elements are such considerations as whether the policeman has identified himself as a peace officer, whether he gave warning that he might shoot, whether he made other serious efforts to capture the escaping person, whether the suspect was wounded or in such physical condition that he could not escape, whether there were other policemen who could surround the suspect, etc.

On the other hand, if the fleeing felon has a reputation for using violence in the past in resisting arrest, if the nature of the crime is physical and dangerous, or if the felon is about to take a position in which he will be able to hold off pursuers, these are valid reasons for the use of deadly force by the police.

In New Hampshire and Rhode Island, they have accepted the Uniform Arrest Act. The law in those states is that there must be a reasonable necessity to use deadly force. Other statutes list as "justifiable homicide" killings by policemen in effecting arrests. In most states, however, it must be necessary to accomplish the arrest.

In a few jurisdictions, by judicial determination, the law imposes a requirement of "absolute" necessity, as compared with "reasonable" necessity, before a policeman can kill an escaping felon. They are Alabama, Kentucky, New York, and perhaps Tennessee.

RIGHT OF A PRIVATE PERSON TO USE FORCE

Only a few states have statutory law covering the right of a private citizen to use force in making an arrest. The laws of Florida, Mississippi, New Mexico, North Dakota, Oklahoma, South Dakota, and Wisconsin, excuse killing by "any person in attempting by lawful ways and means to apprehend any person for any felony committed."

In most states, a private person may not use killing force if the felony is not "atrocious." In North Carolina and Pennsylvania, the courts have held that a private individual may not shoot a felon who is running away if the felony was minor or nonatrocious. However, in Texas, there is an exception by statute if the crime is committed at night, where the identity of the felon may be unknown and therefore his arrest is difficult.

In May of 1966, Clifford G. Miller, Jr., of San Diego, California, was the first person in the United States to receive compensation under a "good Samaritan" law—a California statute passed to indemnify persons who sustained injuries or damages in the course of stopping crimes or catching criminals. Miller had fractured his hand while scuffling with a prisoner.

RIGHT TO USE FORCE IN MISDEMEANOR CASES

In most states, an officer may not ever kill a person who committed a misdemeanor. However, a few jurisdictions have enacted statutory proposals that permit homicide in such a situation: Hawaii, California, and Missouri. There are statutes in other states that seem to indicate that killing may be justified to overcome resistance by one who has committed a misdemeanor, but it would be unwise to rely on them.

USE OF FORCE IN SELF-DEFENSE

A policeman, of course, is entitled to use force in self-defense. If he kills in self-defense, then he may be required to show that he had to use such deadly force to protect himself. Thus, not all the struggling on the part of the person who is being arrested justifies the policeman in using his gun. Of course, in the case of resisting felons, the policeman has the privilege, aside from self-defense, to use deadly force to effect the arrest or to prevent the felon from fleeing, provided that he is reasonable in his belief that a necessity to do so exists.

Even in the case of a misdemeanor, while deadly force is not justified to effect an arrest or prevent an escape, a prolonged struggle may ensue, and the officer may at some point be entitled to shoot in self-defense.

REMEDIES FOR ILLEGAL USE OF FORCE

A policeman may be held liable in the civil court for damages, if he has used an excessive amount of force in arresting, enforcing custody, or recapture. The victim, of course, can protect himself against excessive force, as a matter of self-defense. After the arrest, if any force is used, the police officer may be held liable in damages that stem from his improper conduct.

Suits for false arrest, based upon excessive force or otherwise, are difficult to win. Of 13,000 suits for personal injuries and property damage filed against New York City from July 1, 1963 to July 1, 1964, 326 were suits based upon acts of the police. Over the same period, seventy-two of such claims were settled for a total amount of $232,424.60. Even after a successful verdict, the successful party may find it difficult to satisfy the judgment.

In 1958, in Boston, a Negro named Ammons and a white owner of an automobile had a relatively minor automobile collision. A fight developed, and, several hours later, the white man turned up with six police officers. Mr. Ammons was beaten while Mrs. Ammons was held down by one of the policemen. Mr. and Mrs. Ammons were charged respectively with stealing money from the other driver and with assault and battery. The charges were thrown out in court. The Ammons brought civil suits based upon false arrest against the police and one for trespass against the other driver. A judgment of $7,000 was awarded in June of 1959. To this date, they haven't collected.

Right of the Citizen to Resist Arrest

While interest generally revolves about the right of the policeman to use force, the other aspect is the right of the person being arrested to resist an illegal arrest.

The general rule has always been that it is illegal to fight a lawful arrest. However, the victim of an illegal arrest is usually permitted to use the same force in protecting himself as a policeman could use in arresting a person for a misdemeanor. The victim may not kill the policeman to avoid being arrested, but he can resist force with force in such case and can kill if that is what is necessary to defend himself from the assault. This state of law was justified at one time, since a prisoner might be kept imprisoned a long time and tortured, all before trial. Today, this is not too likely. Resistance to arrest is usually by use of firearms, with great danger to the police. Resistance to arrest is more likely to come from real criminals, rather than innocent citizens. Based upon this rationale, the Uniform Arrest Act does away with the right to resist an illegal arrest by a known policeman. Where the Uniform Arrest Act is law, the person arrested cannot defend himself against a charge of murder, manslaughter, or felonious assault on the ground that resistance was legal because the arrest was illegal. Of course, the defense of self-defense still stands.

The question of how much force is reasonable in any given situation will continue to be a vexing one. Consider the case of Ramsey W. Hall, a graduate student at Vanderbilt University in Nashville, Tennessee. As far as anyone knew, he was an even-tempered and polite young man, although his six feet, two inches and 220 pounds might have given others a different impression. In January of 1966, on the day he was killed by the police, after taking examinations at school, he drove off in his automobile. The following events took place. He received a ticket for speeding from a policeman who later described him as "courteous"; he had an uneventful conference with his English professor. Then he telephoned a young lady whom he did not know very well and, after blurting out that he was "intoxicated with love," proposed marriage to her.

It required a policeman to get him home. Once there, he spoke wildly to his landlady and began to kick at her door. In response to a call, three other police officers appeared on the scene. They attempted to talk to him, but he repulsed them, loudly demanding a search warrant. Suddenly Hall moved to strike the landlady and lashed out at the policemen. A general melee ensued. In the heat of the moment, and before his brother officers could restrain him, one of the policemen drew his service revolver and fired six shots into the youth, mortally wounding him.

The grand jury refused to indict the man who had fired the fatal shots. The officer, who had never used his revolver prior to this episode, said contritely, "I would give anything if this had never happened. I exercised what I felt was my best judgment and I did what I thought I had to do." In this situation, who was wrong?

VII.

Search and Seizure

EVERY PERSON has the need to have some place that he can call his own—a Shangri-La in which he is master and where he can find sanctuary from the pressures and buffeting of modern life. Dr. Aristide H. Esser of the Rockland State Hospital, Orangeburg, New York, in an address delivered to the American Association of Science, has pointed out the importance of this psychological fact.

> Man has an inborn sense of concern about his place in the world. . . . Even in a mental institution the patients try to establish their own identities by occupying a certain place as their own. This may be a chair, a corner of a room, or a corridor. . . . However, some patients do not have the tenacity to defend their territory against intruders. Such patients may wander continually about, finding a place nobody else would like, such as a windowless corner.

As compared with the interest of the individual in the privacy and security of his abode, there must be considered the need of society to invade the "castle" in order to protect the community from those who harbor dangerous or illegal objects. It is in this conflict between the individual right to sanctity and the community's right to protect itself that the principles of the law of search and seizure apply.[1]

Constitutional Development

The idea of the search warrant was fraught with odious connotations in English history and that of colonial America. The indiscriminate use of the Writ of Assistance, which was a catchall search warrant, precipitated the constitutional prohibition of "unreasonable search and seizure." It also led to the specification of the situations and the manner in which search warrants could be used. For a long time, the validity of the search warrant as a legal device was in question, but gradually, subject to many restrictions, its use was permitted by law. Some restrictions on searches and seizures are contained in the United States Constitution and the state constitutions, as well as various statutes. These restrictions prohibit searches and seizures that are "unreasonable," specify the situations in which search warrants are allowed, and detail the requirements for the issuance of a search warrant.

The provision in the Massachusetts Constitution of 1780 was the most broad in operation. It was the model for the Fourth Amendment to the United States Constitution, which states:

> The right of the people to be secure in their persons, homes, papers, and effects, against unreasonable searches and seizures, shall not be violated, and no warrants shall issue, but upon probable cause, supported by oath or affirmation, and particularly observing the place to be searched, and the persons or things to be seized.

Initially, this only restricted the activities of the federal government. Now, the law is clear that the Fourth Amendment also extends to the states.

The Fourth Amendment is sometimes applied to the seizure of persons, by way of arrest, but it is usually regarded as applying to the search and seizure of property. It does not interdict every search and seizure, nor does it demand a warrant in every case. Yet the Fourth Amendment does require that if a person or his property is to be searched or seized without a warrant, then such an act must be reasonable and on some justifiable basis.

It should be noted, however, that the United States Constitution and the state constitutions, as well, apply only to the acts by agents of the government. They do not prohibit a *private* person from making a search and seizure, whether reasonable or unreasonable. While the federal government, the states, or local units of government may not pass laws authorizing unreasonable searches or seizures, they may enact laws permitting searches and seizures within limits and may adopt reasonable regulations covering them.

Meaning of Search and Seizure

The word "search" in the phrase "search and seizure" means the examination of a person's abode or person in the attempt to find property that is illegal or stolen or that constitutes some evidence of that person's guilt of some criminal act. In the same context, the word "seizure" means that property is taken away by force from the person in possession of it and without that person's consent. A search and seizure is frequently made pursuant to a search warrant. A search warrant is a written order, signed by a judge, which directs a policeman, peace officer, or someone else, to look for specified personal property and bring it before the court for use in criminal prosecution.

The law is that objects that are visible cannot be the subject of a search. This is so even if these objects are not available physically. Thus, if the policeman looks in through a glass window or door from the outside of a building, and objects are seen by him, this is not a search. Even where observation is made through a keyhole or other aperture that has not been expressly opened by the police, the courts generally hold that there has been no search. But where the police have constructed a peephole or other opening in order to see, it is generally considered a physical intrusion and therefore a search in the contemplation of the law.

The use of a searchlight or binoculars does not convert the situation into a search. In one case, the Supreme Court decided that flashing a flashlight beam from one boat to another to make observations was not a search. Another case, in California, involved observation by a policeman at an amusement park pay toilet. There, a pipe came through the roof of a comfort station. When it was uncapped, the officer could look into two of the toilet stalls. After diligent attention to duty, the policeman was able to see persons committing allegedly homosexual acts. Even though the police had not installed the pipe and the removal of the cover was outside the premises proper, the police surveillance was deemed an illegal search. The court held that this was a "fishing expedition" to find criminal activity. The person using the stall was entitled to as much privacy as if he were at home, even though this was a pay toilet in an amusement park open to the public.

Search and Seizure in the Electronic Age

Today, it is no longer necessary to invade a person's home physically in order to know what is going on inside. By the means of electronic techniques, such as wiretapping, it is easy to breach the sanctity of any person's abode without opening a door or a window. There has been controversy as to whether such eavesdropping constitutes a violation of federal or state constitutional provisions or legislation concerning this subject.

The Supreme Court of the United States has decided that wiretapping does not violate the Fourth Amendment to the Constitution. In one case, the Supreme Court decided that a concealed wire recorder used by an Internal Revenue agent was not a violation of a person's right of privacy under the Constitution.

Yet, a federal statute prohibits the disclosure of information obtained by intercepting interstate communications such as telephone conversations. And the Supreme Court has recognized that, since the Fourth Amendment prohibits unjustified invasions of privacy of one's home, this order covers electronic devices, as well as physical invasions. On December 18, 1967, by *Katz* v. *United States,* the Supreme Court clearly authorized electronic eavesdropping by the police. At the same time, the Court extended the reach of the Fourth Amendment by holding that a warrant must be obtained in advance, even when the police plan to eavesdrop on persons in semipublic places, such as telephone booths.

The extent to which information derived from the use of electronic devices may be introduced as evidence in trials is not entirely clear and is changing rapidly. Generally, it is fair to say that evidence based on wiretapping is excluded in federal courts because of the laws of Congress, rather than as a matter of constitutional prohibition. In the states, the rule is even less certain. Usually, evidence illegally obtained by a person other than a police officer is not admissable in court, but evidence secured by a policeman will ordinarily be admitted, even though obtained illegally. It seems likely that the rules of evidence with respect to wiretapping and other types of eavesdropping through electronic devices will be in a state of flux for some time.[2]

SEARCH AND SEIZURE WITHOUT A WARRANT

It is noteworthy that a search conducted by a law-enforcement agent may infringe upon the interests of more than one person. As an example, if a person sends a messenger with an article of personal property and a policeman searches that messenger, it may be that the messenger cannot claim that his rights of privacy have been infringed if the object of personal property is examined. Yet, it may be argued that the search violates his constitutional rights as well as those of the owner of the article.

An owner of premises that are illegally searched may, paradoxically, not have a constitutional right against such invasion. The simplest illustration would be the situation in which the police broke into a leased apartment and searched it without legal basis. There, the tenant, who does not actually own the building, may be entitled to the constitutional protection, but not the landlord. A similiar situation may obtain where a desk used by an employee at his place of employment is searched by the police upon permission of the employer. Since the desk was made available to the employee for his own use, the right to consent to search this desk was not for the employer, but rather the employee alone.

Only the person whose premises are invaded may claim the protection of the Constitution. If the police illegally break into one man's home and find evidence of a crime perpetrated by another man, the latter cannot claim that such evidence cannot be used against him. And, at the same time, the owner of the premises, assuming he was not involved in the crime himself, cannot ask for the suppression of this evidence.

It should be kept in mind that the Constitution protects hardened and known criminals from unreasonable searches and seizures, just as is protects anyone else. Corporations, too, are entitled to the protection of the Fourth Amendment. However, courts are more ready to permit examination of corporate property than property belonging to individuals. The rationale is that the corporation is a creature of the state, and that a condition precedent of its existence is accountability for its acts. This is even more convincing when the business of the corporation is "affected with a public interest," such as telephone or electric service. All individuals and corporations within the jurisdiction of the United States are owed protection under the Fourth Amendment.[3]

Public Records

Where, as a condition of being granted a license, or because public safety requries it, or for some other reason, the law imposes the obligation that records be kept, these are considered public records. As such they may be required to be available for inspection. They are not protected by the Fourth Amendment. An example is a pharmacist who is ordered by regulation to keep a record of all prescriptions of narcotics. He cannot refuse to permit the law-enforcement agents to inspect these records. However, the agents cannot come at any hour and demand the right to plow through all the records. The search must be made at a reasonable time. Furthermore, the search itself must be a reasonable one.

Frisking

At common law, the policeman had no right to search a suspected person before arresting him. But this left the policeman at the mercy of anyone he simply stopped to question if that person had a concealed deadly weapon. The Uniform Arrest Act legalizes "frisking." Under this Act, a peace officer may search any person he has stopped, to search for a dangerous weapon, whenever he has a reasonable basis for believing he is in such danger. If the policeman finds a weapon, he may retain it until the questioning has been completed. At that time, he must either return it or arrest the person. After a valid arrest, a policeman has the authority to search his prisoner. This rationale certainly applies to "frisking." The American Law Institute, which is considering a model code of pre-arraignment procedure, has proposed a rule permitting "stop and frisk" action by the police.[4]

Search Following a Lawful Arrest

A search is authorized without a warrant when a person has been legally arrested for a crime. At that point, the police may search him to discover if he has a weapon, burglar tools, or stolen goods. At times, the premises where he was arrested my be subjected to search.

In 1962, two private citizens pursued an armed thief to the house into which they had seen him run. They then called the police. When the officers arrived, Mrs. Bennie Joe Hayden permitted them to enter. They found Hayden in his bed, with no clothes on, and they subsequently discovered his clothing—and two guns—in the washing machine. Hayden's ultimate conviction was based upon the identification of his clothing by several eyewitnesses of the crime.

Under the rule that existed before the Hayden case, only four kinds of evidence could be seized by the police: the proceeds of a crime; the tools by means of which a crime was committed; the objects that made an escape possible; and items that are essentially illegal contraband, such as narcotics. Nothing else could be seized, since no other object was permitted to be used as evidence.

In the Hayden case, however, the Supreme Court rejected this rule, holding that the yield of a reasonable search may be used as legal evidence to convict an accused.[5]

The rule has always been that the policeman can search the person of anyone validly arrested and seize evidence of the crime for which the arrest has been made, illegal property, or weapons. Situations in which the suspect is physically examined include such cases as drunken driving, rape, and narcotics use or possession. The examination may legally include a rectal examination, drunkometer test, fluoroscope examination, or blood sampling. The right to search an individual has been construed to authorize examination of his clothing, the insides of his pockets, and other things "in his immediate control."

A search of premises without a warrant is invalid if the arrest was made elsewhere. The constitutional guarantee extends only to a "house." Although there is no universal agreement, the courts generally include a garage and contiguous garden as part of the house. The federal view is that the house need be occupied at the time of the search in order to secure constitutional protection. Places of business such as an office, store, or factory seem to be protected, as well as hotel rooms, if used, even on a casual basis, as a home.

However, the right to search without a warrant as incident to a

gal arrest does not allow the policeman to tear the house apart.
owever, the tendency has been to permit the policeman more lati-
de in going through closed drawers and closets, assuming the search
valid to begin with.

utomobiles and Other Vehicles

What appears to be an exception to the requirement of a search
arrant is the authority of police officers to halt an automobile and
arch it. This may be permissible because automobiles may be moved
sily and quickly from place to place, making it impossible to go to
urt and return with a search warrant in time. In a Supreme Court
se, prohibition agents were carrying on an investigation. They
orked out an arrangement to buy illegal liquor from the suspected
dividual. The agents managed to secure the description of his auto-
obile and its license number. Several months later they noticed the
r and saw that it seemed to be weighed down. They halted the car
d upon searching it, discovered sixty-eight bottles of liquor. The
urt decided that the search and seizure was legal, relying on the
planation that there was a legimate distinction between requiring a
arrant to search a stationary house and allowing a search without a
arrant in the case of an automobile. It should be remembered that,
en in such situations, there must exist a "probable cause" to search.
The same relaxation of the rules relating to the need for a warrant
search applies to boats and other media of transportation, because
the mobility of the vehicle.[6]

onsent

If an individual has unquestionably given his consent to a search
d seizure, no warrant is necessary. He has waived his rights under
e Fourth Amendment. If the individual gives this consent because he
compelled to do so by the police, or because he does not know that
can legally resist the search and seizure, the consent does not stand
. In a key case,[7] the Court stated: "Entry to the defendant's living
arters, which was the beginning of the search, was demanded under
lor of office. It was granted in submission to authority rather than as
understanding and intentional waiver of a constitutional right." In
at case, the court found that consent had not been given, and there-
re the Fourth Amendment prohibited the search.

SEARCH AND SEIZURE WITH A WARRANT

The Constitution does not prohibit searches and seizures when there
a warrant, but a search warrant, like a warrant of arrest, must meet
e requirements of the Fourth Amendment. The warrant can be
sued only upon "probable cause" and it must describe with specifi-

city what is to be searched or seized. The warrant cannot authoriz
"fishing expedition." It is legal process directed by a court to sec
specific evidence to be used in a prosecution for a crime, which
that time has been committed. In general, the search warrant may
employed in all those situations in which a valid search and seizur
permissible. The requirements for the issuance of a search warr
are usually specific by statute. If they are met, the court may th
direct that the search be made and certain property be seized.

If the search warrant is not issued by the proper officer, it is inval
Under federal legislation the search warrant must be issued by
United States District Court Judge, or a judge of a state or ter
torial court of record, or by a United States Commissioner for the d
trict where the search is to be made. In the states, the right to iss
a warrant is provided by statute and is generally restricted to a memb
of the judiciary.

The leading case dealing with the subject is *Mapp* v. *Ohio*. It
cided that all evidence secured by searches and seizures in violati
of the federal Constitution is inadmissible in a criminal trial held
a state court.

On May 23, 1957, three policemen demanded admittance to t
home of Dollree Mapp, located in Cleveland, Ohio. She telephon
her lawyer and, on his advice, refused to let them in. Several hou
later, the number of policemen was increased to seven, and they bro
into Miss Mapp's home. They did not permit Miss Mapp's attorn
to come into the house or to speak with her. It is questionable wheth
the policeman had a search warrant. Their reason for trying to get
was information that there was a person "hiding out in the house wh
was wanted for questioning in connection with a recent bombing, a
that there was a large amount of policy paraphernalia being hidd
in the house." The missing "person" and the gambling "paraphe
nalia" were never found. The case is a landmark in reasserting the rig
of a person to be secure in his home from unwarranted arrest, as w
as "unreasonable" search and seizure.[8]

Application for a Search Warrant

The search warrant has to be grounded on a firm factual bas
Thus, its application is made on the basis of an affidavit or complair
under oath or affirmation, the facts of which support the need for th
warrant. The entire complaint or affidavit is to be considered in dete

ining its efficacy. The statutory requirements as to number of affidavits and credibility must be met. There is no rigid rule as to when the application for the warrant must be made, but it must be within a reasonable period of time after the commission of the alleged offense.

The complaint or affidavit must comply either absolutely or in substance with the requirements of constitution or statute in regard to form. This includes such elements as date, signature and seal of affiant, the oath, and the description of the property to be seized.

The essence of the affidavit is compliance with legal requirement that probable cause for the search warrant must be complied with before the warrant can be issued. "Probable cause" is a phrase that has a long legal history. For this reason its definition is hard to pin down. It has been defined as "the existence of such facts and circumstances as would excite an honest belief in a reasonable mind, acting on all the facts and circumstances within the knowledge of the magistrate, that the charge made by the applicant for the warrant is true." The requirement of "probable cause" seems to be about the equivalent of "reasonable cause."

Obviously, the judge should decide whether or not to issue the warrant as soon as possible after the application is made. The warrant generally may be issued at the home of the judge and at any hour.

Execution of a Search Warrant

The search warrant must be executed by the officer, or category of officers, enumerated in the warrant. Of course, they must have the inherent authority to act. They may be assisted by anyone whom they ask for help, even though the assistants are not named in the warrant. The warrant must be executed within the time set or, if no time is fixed, then within a reasonable period of time. It is more appropriate that the warrant be executed in the daytime. However, by legislation, and in some special cases in the absence of legislation, a warrant may be executed at night. Where the warrant does not authorize service at night, then it must be served during the day. The policeman acting pursuant to a warrant may search the person or location and seize the object only if so specified in the warrant. The policeman may not under the warrant search any other residence or location or remove any other object.

The policeman should usually serve the warrant on the person in charge of the place to be searched, or at least show it or read aloud what it provides. If the person accused is not present, the police officer can proceed with the search and seizure. If the policeman makes a demand for admission and he is turned down, he may forcibly enter and seize the property.

If the house is unoccupied, the demand or notice is not necessary In 1964, the "knock, knock" proposal was enacted into law in New York. It authorizes a judge issuing a search warrant to dispense with the requirement that a policeman executing the warrant identify himself and state his purpose for entering. The law provides for an officer's breaking into a room unannounced if the judge is satisfied that the property sought may be readily destroyed by the suspect or that making the announcement would endanger the officer.

There is a requirement that the police officer must execute the warrant with a high degree of care and no abuse. He is required to avoid damage to the property, if possible, in the course of making his investigation. The policeman must leave the premises as soon as he has discharged his responsibility under the warrant. If he exceeds his authority, he is answerable for his illegal acts, but his acts are invalid only to the extent that they exceed authority. The failure of the policeman to make a report or return to the court after the excution of the warrant as required is not deemed to invalidate the search and seizure

Remedies for an Illegal Search or Seizure

A number of alternative methods of procedure are available to a person who feels that he is being subjected to an illegal search and seizure. It should be noted that, under federal law, the question of whether "probable cause" has been established before the warrant was issued may be tested. In most state courts, if the warrant is valid on its face, and the affidavit is sufficient on its face, the statements of the petitions cannot be re-examined. As a consequence, the determination, made by the judge issuing the warrant, that the probable cause existed, will not be reviewed.

A person whose property has been illegally seized is generally entitled to have his property returned to him. If the property is of the nature that possession itself is illegal, such as a pistol, it will not be returned. But if it is not of this type, it will be held so long as necessary for the prosecution and then returned. If a reasonable time has elapsed without its return, then application should be made for return If the application is denied, then a lawsuit may be instituted for the return of the object or money damages.

CIVIL LIABILITY

If the legitimate rights of an individual against an unreasonable search and seizure have been breached, he becomes entitled to redress. A judge who issues a search warrant without having jurisdiction over the application may be liable. A policeman who effects an illegal search and seizure may be liable. He will be protected if the warrant

ppears legal on its face. But the policeman is bound to execute a
warrant in a legal manner, and he is liable if his acts in executing
the warrant are contrary to law. An individual who causes a warrant
o be issued out of malice and in the absence of actual probable cause
will be liable. Persons who are not authorized to execute the warrant
and who do so may be liable. But it should be remembered that one
who executes a warrant under the authority of a police officer, in
good faith, is generally not liable. Of course, such defenses as consent
o the search or waiver are good defenses to an action for illegal search
and seizure.

CRIMINAL LIABILITY

At common law, a wrongful search and seizure was not a crime.
But today, by statute, policemen and others may be made responsible
and punishable under the criminal law for illegal searches and seizures.

EXCLUSION FROM EVIDENCE

To be meaningful, the search and seizure provisions of the Fourth
Amendment must be enforced. The civil and criminal remedies, as
well as the possibility of administrative proceedings against the law-
enforcement agent, are of limited value for this purpose.

The courts have evolved another technique—the exclusionary rule
—stating that evidence procured in violation of the Fourth Amendment may not permitted as evidence in court. The underlying theory
is that, if the evidence obtained by an unconstitutional search and
seizure cannot be introduced in court, then policemen will find no
reason to search and seize by illegal means.

VIII.

Illegal Detention and Remedies

DETENTION BEFORE ARREST

FROM TIME TO TIME a person will be stopped by a policeman and asked a few questions. Less freqently such interrogation, before an arrest, may be for a longer period. Such detention has been practiced to facilitate investigation. It has been employed in the United States and in England, as well. This method is used because the police have to work quickly, and it saves time in securing information.

It may be argued that there is a substantial difference between detention and arrest, that the individual who is being held for questioning is not treated as a prisoner; he is not put in a cell, but waits in a waiting room. He is fed and treated well by the police. But the "detained" are, indeed, at times subjected to abuse. The person who is "requested" to accompany the policeman to the station house to be detained usually must accede to the request and is not permitted to leave at his will. In Continental Europe, however, distinction has been drawn between arrest and detention. There is no requirement of a charge being made, nor a necessity for a reasonable ground of suspicion that the person detained has committed a crime.

Interrogation, without immediate arrest, appears to be important for effective police work. The American Law Institute in its Draft Model Code of Pre-Arraignment Procedure has proposed a short period of on-the-spot detention of suspects and witnesses and the use of "nondeadly" force to enforce such detention if necessary, in situations where there is reasonable cause to believe an offense has been committed, or in "suspicious circumstances." This detention cannot exceed twenty minutes.

DETENTION AFTER ARREST

Unnecessary Delay

Even after a person is arrested, the police are restricted in their

76

egal authority to detain him. In every jurisdiction, federal and state, law-enforcement officers are obliged to keep the period of detention between arrest and preliminary examination before the court as short as possible. The test is usually that an arrested person be brought before the judge for a preliminary examination "without delay." Although the test is uniformly stated in this phrase, the courts have interpreted it in different ways. However, the Supreme Court of the United States has ruled that the preliminary hearing must take place very shortly after the arrest, usually within a few hours.

In a leading case, the Court ruled that where the accused was not brought before a United States Commissioner for a preliminary hearing for nine hours, and in that interval he confessed to the federal police, the confession could not be admitted into evidence. The Supreme Court has made it clear that, even if the confession is voluntary, the illegal detention invalidates the confession in the federal courts.

The attitude of the courts in some of the states is in sharp contrast. In 1952, the Supreme Court of New Jersey ruled that, although a detention of nine days between the time of arrest and the preliminary examination, "without satisfactory explanation, is a violation of . . . (the judicial rule) which requires an officer making an arrest to take the arrested person 'without unnecessary delay' before the court or magistrate, it does not of itself establish or constitute a denial of due process which would invalidate the conviction."[1]

The fact that the policeman broke the law of New Jersey by detaining the subject did not require the confession or conviction to be set aside.

What is perhaps more important, certainly to a person who is illegally detained, is what the police practices are with respect to detention, rather than the judicial rules regarding the time lag before the preliminary hearing or examination.

Incommunicado Detention

Some local or state law-enforcement agents segregate persons who are arrested from friends or relatives or lawyer, especially when it is felt such communication will prevent preparation for the prosecution.

A single example will illustrate the problem. On June 30, 1958, the Supreme Court of the United States, rendered a verdict in a case that involved a New Jersey prisoner.[2] Vincent Cincencia had been implicated in a murder. His lawyer suggested that he turn himself in at the station house. He went there with his father and his brother. What happened to him is best described in the words of the Supreme Court of the United States:

Upon arrival at the Orange police station at 9:00 A.M. on December 18, 1947, petitioner was separated from the others and taken by detectives to the Newark Police headquarters. At approximately 2:00 P.M. the same day, petitioner's father, brother, and Mr. Palmieri, the lawyer, arrived at the Newark station. Mr. Palmieri immediately asked to see the petitioner, but this request was refused by police. He repeated this request at intervals throughout the afternoon and well into the evening, but without success. During this period, petitioner, who was being questioned intermittently by the police, asked to see his lawyer. These requests were also denied. Lawyer and client were not permitted to confer until 9:30 P.M. by which time petitioner had made and signed a written confession to . . . murder.

According to Cincencia's lawyer, two entreaties to be permitted to see his client were turned down. He claims that the police were blunt enough to say, "We're working on him."

However, because the police were not federal officers, the Court did not reverse the conviction on the grounds that there had been unnecessary delay.

Detention and the Third Degree

Apparently the police do detain many persons and hold them for short periods of time—to "cool them down," to question them, and to "teach them a lesson," and then let them go. This is serious, but there is a more serious aspect to illegal detention. Illegal detention and the forced confession often go hand in hand. A prisoner who is detained for a period of time before the preliminary examination by a judge can still defend himself at the trial. But if, during the period of detention, he is forced to confess, his defense is virtually gone long before he begins his trial. A study by the Illinois Division of the American Civil Liberties Union reported that "the practice of third degree methods . . . [is] almost always the fruit of lengthy, secret detentions."[3] Other authorities share this opinion.

DEVELOPMENT OF REMEDIES

A cornerstone of the struggle for civil liberties in England and America has been the concern with preventing unlawful detentions of private citizens by the authorities. The remedies have taken two forms. The first is a judicial proceeding to secure the release of the private citizen held, known as habeas corpus. The second is an action to recompense the person detained by way of money damages.

Habeas Corpus

The term "habeas corpus" is familiar to almost everyone. As translated from the Latin, it literally means, "you are ordered to have the body." If a relative or lawyer of a person who has been arrested feels that he is being improperly held, a writ of habeas corpus is obtained. This writ, or order, commands the police authorities to bring the arrested individual into the court. When that person is produced before the court, the judge decides whether or not there is sufficient legal basis to keep him in jail.

Habeas corpus is recognized as "the highest remedy in law for any man that is imprisoned." Its foundation was established in 1215, in the English Magna Charta. Its usefulness against false imprisonment was tested in the last part of the seventeenth century. Since then it has been a significant weapon against tyranny in English-speaking countries.

Although habeas corpus may be used in cases of private, unlawful detention, such as where a wife is imprisoned by a husband or there is a conflict over the custody of a child, its principal use is against wrongful detention by the police. It works this way: The police officer arrests a person who he believes has committed a crime. The person who is arrested, or a friend, has a lawyer apply to a judge for a writ of habeas corpus. The writ commands that the police must appear in court with the prisoner. If there are no legal charges to place against him, the prisoner must be released.

Habeas corpus is designed to free a person wrongfully held. If a person has been arrested and unlawfully detained he may subsequently sue for damages. As a general matter, it may be said that a policeman or the arresting authority who wrongfully holds a person is liable for the false imprisonment.

BASIS IN CONSTITUTION AND STATUTE

The right to habeas corpus is contained in the Constitution of the United States. It provides that:

> The Privilege of the Writ of Habeas Corpus shall not be suspended unless, when in Cases of Rebellion or Invasion, the public safety may require it.

This is directed to situations in which the federal authorities are concerned. However, through interpretation by the courts of the Fourteenth Amendment to the federal Constitution, the writ is available against state and other local police. In addition, the constitution of many states contain this protection. However, for the most part today the legal provisions concerning the writ of habeas corpus are set out in state statutes. The state legislatures cannot cut down this basic constitutional right, but they can establish reasonable regulation for the use of habeas corpus or grant broader protection than the constitutions provide. In some states, even without statutes, rights are recognized relating to habeas corpus by certain judges.

INVOKING HABEAS CORPUS

The essential purpose of the writ of habeas corpus is to provide an immediate hearing for a person who is detained, to find out whether the restraint is an illegal one. Usually, the federal courts will not issue a writ of habeas corpus to decide whether a person detained by state or other law authorities should be released. Whether or not any court will issue the writ is usually within the discretion of the court and it will not be issued where the prisoner does not need the help or where the writ could not help him. It follows that if the petitioner has some other legal remedy that can give him adequate relief—if the proceedings are still pending or he has an available appeal—the writ will not be issued. A precondition for habeas corpus is that the person be actually restrained. It will not be issued for this reason where the petitioner is out on bail or where he has voluntarily surrendered

NATURE OF ILLEGAL DETENTION

The right to habeas corpus is based upon the illegality of restraint at the time of filing the petition. It does not depend upon the defendant's innocence or guilt. The writ of habeas corpus may be issued where there is a denial of opportunity to give bail or where there is a delay in taking the prisoner before the judge. It may be granted if the court that issued the warrant was without jurisdiction. It may be issued where the crime for which the person was held is not in fact a crime in law. It may be issued, in some states, where the court finds that the statute under which the petitioner is restrained is unconstitutional. This is also the rule where the person detained is entitled to an immunity from arrest.

HABEAS CORPUS IN SPECIAL CASES

Usually, the writ of habeas corpus is appropriate to determine the validity of an order by which an alien is being detained while a decision is being made as to whether he should be admitted into the

United States. As a precondition, however, the alien must exhaust those remedial procedures available to him under the appropriate statute, and the writ itself only seeks answers to a few basic questions. Thus, if the alien was afforded a full and fair hearing with an opportunity to state his position and present his evidence, and then the decision based on evidence was made and confirmed by the investigating agency, then the order will stand. In deportation cases, the courts will usually not review the administrative decision. The habeas corpus inquiry will be limited to whether there was a full and fair hearing, whether the determination was based on sure evidence and not arbitrary, or whether it resulted from a mistaken rule of law.

The writ may be invoked under certain circumstances to obtain the freedom of a soldier, sailor, or even civilian illegally restrained by the military authorities.

Although habeas corpus may be granted where the person held is illegally denied an opportunity to seek bail, it is not appropriate to secure the freedom of a person who did not raise the bail set. It is appropriate in a situation in which the bail required is excessive or where the jailed person has posted the required bail but has not been released. If a person is properly held in contempt of court, he may not secure his release through a writ of habeas corpus. It may also be brought to obtain the release of one held for the purpose of extradition to another state or country. However, a person who is arrested for the purpose of extradition has the burden of overcoming the prima-facie presumption that the custody is lawful. The writ of habeas corpus has been used to determine the validity of the arrest of persons under quarantine or health regulations, enemy aliens, and others.

NATURE OF THE HABEAS CORPUS PROCEEDING

The nature of the habeas corpus proceeding varies in detail from jurisdiction to jurisdiction. For the most part, these details are prescribed by legislation, federal and state. Since the habeas corpus proceeding relates to fundamental rights of individuals, the courts have been liberal in permitting deviations by the petitioner from the prescribed requirements of such statutes.

The time within which an application for a writ of habeas corpus must be made is not rigidly prescribed. Usually, the writ of habeas corpus is initiated by means of an application or petition to the appropriate court by the prisoner or someone who is acting for him. The writ may be sought by a prisoner who feels that he is being improperly detained. It may be brought by someone acting in his behalf, and it may be brought by one who has a legitimate reason for being interested, such as a lawyer, friend, relative, or guardian. The application can be made without the consent or even the knowledge of the prisoner. However, a stranger should not apply for the release of a prisoner on habeas corpus. This might be against the best interests of the person detained, in situations in which the petitioner might be hostile to him or wish to "silence" him. The person who has the power to produce the prisoner and in whose custody he is being held is the person against whom the writ of habeas corpus is sought. He is called the *respondent*. In addition to the petitioner, the person being detained (if he is not the petitioner) and the respondent are the parties to the proceeding. Other parties may be permitted to intervene if the court feels that such parties have a legitimate interest in the application. An example of such a party would be the American Liberties Union or the N.A.A.C.P.

The proceeding is initiated by a petition that presents to the court the claims of the prisoner. It names the people involved, the place of detention, and the basis on which the claim of improper imprisonment is based.

Usually, the court will require that there must be attached to the petition a copy of the record of alleged illegal procedure or the legal order or warrant that authorizes the detention of the prisoner. It is generally provided that the petition must be verified under oath.

When the writ of habeas corpus is served, the person to whom it is directed is expected to make some answer, called the *return*. In the return it should be stated whether the person in question is in the custody of the respondent or whether he has been transferred to some other place. If the return acknowledges custody of the prisoner, it should then state the basis for the imprisonment. If the basis for the detention is a written document, a copy should be attached to the return.

Usually, with the return, the respondent should produce the prisoner, in person, before the court or judge that issued the writ. The judge or court may permit the prisoner to furnish bail while it is resolving the problems presented by the habeas corpus proceeding. The court will hold a hearing and, on the basis of the testimony and the documents submitted, will reach a determination.

After the hearing, the judge will either validate the detention, release the person, or permit him to supply bail, as he thinks appropriate. If the court refuses to discharge the prisoner, this does not bar a subsequent application for a writ of habeas corpus. But the second court may take the first turn-down into account in deciding.

Usually, a policeman, or his superior, or the municipality may be

Actions in Damages for Illegal Detention

deemed liable for an illegal detention where there has been a failure to take the prisoner before a court within a reasonable time, or where the prisoner is denied an opportunity to give bail, or where other circumstances of this type exist.

The fact that the person sued has acted upon orders from his superior does not give him an excuse for not bringing the arrested person before the proper official without unreasonable delay. The law is not consistent in answering the question of whether once one policeman turns the prisoner over to the custody of another, the former is then excused for subsequent detention. There are some cases that go as far as to say that the arresting officer is liable where there has been unreasonable delay in taking the prisoner before the judge or for the purpose of having bail fixed, although the original arrest was lawful.

The issue as to what is an "unreasonable delay" in a suit for damages is not easy to solve. It is generally considered a question of fact to be resolved by a jury. It is possible, under some circumstances, for a comparatively short delay, of perhaps an hour or less, to be considered "unreasonable." The delay may be considered excusable if the judge was not available, or if the policeman who had custody of the prisoner was tied up with other duties, or if the prisoner himself was in a physical or emotional condition so as to dictate delay.

However, where the delay was caused by the desire on the part of the police authorities to pursue their investigation, this is not permissible, if it is considered "unreasonable."

The prisoner may waive his right to be released promptly or not to be arrested. He may agree to be detained pending a police investigation or he may relinquish his right to be brought before a judge within a reasonable period of time, if he is discharged.

Special Status of Habeas Corpus

Recently, the Supreme Court has underlined the special status of the Great Writ. Not only can a prisoner invoke it to test a sentence he has not as yet begun to serve, but he can attack through federal habeas corpus a conviction under which he has completed his sentence before the final determination of his appeal.[4] And an unchallenged consecutive sentence that would not commence until the completion of the sentence does not bar habeas corpus.[5]

IX.

Release Before Trial — The Right to Bail

A PERSON WHO IS ARRESTED and detained has the right to apply for release pending trial. This application generally asks for the person to be released from jail, if an amount of money or other valuables be left with the appropriate official to ensure that the released person will come back to appear in court when requested. In the case of certain minor offenses, the police may release the arrested person on bail. In other cases, the bail is set by a judge.

A fundamental problem in the administration of justice has been the question of what to do with the person accused of criminal conduct between the time of arrest and the date scheduled for his trial. Other complex sociolegal problems also present pressing questions. Is every arrested person entitled to be released pending trial if he can give adequate assurance that he will be available for trial? Is it a valid basis for denying bail that the accused man may engage in criminal activity if released between the date of his arrest and the date set for trail? If the judge setting bail has reasonable assurance that the accused will appear in court when required, can bail be set at a high figure because of the seriousness of the alleged crime or the circumstances under which it is committed? Since bail involves furnishing money or other property, is this not illegal discrimination against an accused who happens to be poor? Does the bail bondsman have a legitimate role in the system of pretrial release?

As early as the days of Plato, it was expressly recognized that bail is a legal device that society uses to insure that an accused will be available for trial and at the same time protect his freedom, since he may ultimately be found innocent of any wrongdoing. "Unless the right to bail before trial is preserved, the presumption of innocence, secured only after centuries of struggle, would lose its meaning."

Theoretically, the rules of release before trial in America are extremely liberal. In England, the fear that the accused will engage in criminal conduct during the period of release is a valid legal basis for denying bail. And, in continental Europe, bail may be legally denied where there exists "a danger that the accused may, by destroying material or evidence of the offense or by influencing witnesses or accomplices, make it more difficult to ascertain the truth."

In the United States, it is universally recognized that the sole and solitary purpose for bail is to insure that the accused will be available to stand trial. The highest court in the State of New York has stated it thus: "The amount must be no more than is necessary to guarantee [the accused's] presence at the trial." And the Supreme Court of the United States has said that bail was designed to give "assurance of the presence of the accused."

There are two preliminary propositions of the law regarding bail. The first proposition is that there exists an absolute right to have bail fixed after arrest and before trial in all noncapital cases. The second proposition is that bail cannot be required in an excessive amount. From the time of the first session of Congress, the law has recognized the right to bail. This right has been consistently recognized in the federal courts. In approximately forty states, the state constitutions establish bail as a matter of right in all cases except those in which the punishment is death, or, in some states, the specific crimes of murder or treason. However, the United States Constitution and the New York State Constitution have no express guarantee of bail. Three states have established a limited right to bail by statute.

The United States Constitution, through the provisions of the Bill of Rights, and the constitutions of every state, except Illinois, include the rule that excessive bail shall not be set. The Eighth Amendment of the federal Constitution provides, in the same phrasing as in the English Bill of Rights, that "excessive bail shall not be required." The Constitution of the State of New York contains the same provision.

The interrelationship between the federal and state constitutional provisions concerning bail have never been finally settled. Technically, the first ten amendments to the federal Constitution, the Bill of Rights, are limitations on the federal government, not on the individual states. Yet, as we have seen in Chapter Four, "The Constitution in the Police Station," a number of the provisions of the Bill of Rights have been construed as being part of the due process clause of the Fourteenth Amendment and, hence, limitations on the states. In a key case, the court's opinion indicated that it "took it for granted" that the prohibition against excessive bail contained in the federal Constitution applied to both federal and state systems.

Most accused persons in the United States have what is, practically speaking, a right to be released on bail. In New York itself, bail cannot be denied on an arbitrary basis. The upper courts in New York have been careful to protect the rights of accused persons to bail.

Even though the appellate courts are sympathetic to the pleas of those who seek bail, this is not the best solution to their plight. Time is often of the essence, especially to one languishing in jail. Appeals cost money, a commodity that may be in short supply to the accused. At the same time, liberalization·of bail provision does not seem to threaten official administration of criminal justice.

THE BAIL SYSTEM

The present method of fixing bail has been studied and restudied. It has been recognized that the system has serious drawbacks. A person who is arrested and is not in a position to provide the necessary money, property, or bond for the bail is not released. Although he may be innocent and may be, in fact, proven innocent after trial, he may feel deprived of treatment equal to that afforded a more affluent person.

Authority to Set Bail

Any court or judge who has the authority to try a defendant in a criminal case has the authority to release him and hence to admit him to bail. If the authority to admit to bail is *not* inherent in the judge or court, then it does not exist, unless expressly granted by statute. Thus, if the judge of a particular court does not have the authority to hold a trial of a particular criminal offense, he cannot set bail in such a case, unless he is authorized to do so specifically by statute.

Usually, nonjudicial officers are not authorized to admit to bail, but they may accept or take bail. However, in some places, nonjudicial officials may fix bail and accept it. As an example, policemen or other peace officers usually may do neither. In some states, however, by statute, peace officers have been given such legal powers. This is also true with respect to court clerks.

The legal authority to admit to bail cannot be delegated to another person, unless it is authorized by statute. However, once the defendant has been admitted to bail by the proper judge or court, the task of accepting the bail bond pursuant to the order is deemed to be an administration act that can be delegated, even without express approval by statute.

Mode of Application for Bail

The procedure for admission to bail is generally established by the rules of the court or by statute. The procedure must be adhered to, but minor deviations can be overlooked. Usually, it is not essential that the defendant or his sponsor or bondsman appear in court or go before the judge at the time the bail is considered, unless the statute requires it or the judge deems it advisable.

The defendant may take action to secure bail by a petition for a writ of habeas corpus or by an application for bail without respect to habeas corpus. The petition or application should set forth facts that would entitle the petitioner to bail, if the facts are true. Where the accused person has been arrested for a bailable offence, he should have the chance to ask bail to be set without delay after his arrest. The only question to be considered by the judge who is hearing the petition is whether the defendant should or should not be admitted to bail. The court should not decide the merits of the case. It should consider all relevant and material evidence mentioned by both parties, if permissible under the rules of evidence. In some states, the court may examine the minutes of the grand jury, in other states it may not.

The order that authorizes the bail should set out the crime charged, the amount of the bail, and in other respects substantially comply with the requirements of the statute. Generally, the authorization or denial of bail may be taken up on appeal, and therefore it is important to have a proper record. Usually the appellate court will not interfere with the discretion of the lower court when that court has abused its discretion.

Source of Bail

The rationale behind the requirement of bail is the fear or the unwillingness on the part of the released prisoner to forfeit the money or property which has been "put up" by him, or someone on his behalf, to guarantee his appearance. If the arrested person has supplied his own bail, upon his failure to appear he loses his own money. If the money or a bond has been furnished by a professional bail bondsman, upon a forfeiture because of nonappearance the bondsman will have a claim for what he has lost against the defendant who has absented himself. The law recognizes a legal obligation on the part of the defendant to indemnify the bondsman if the surety is required to pay upon the failure of the released prisoner to appear. If the cash or the property is supplied by a relative or a friend, or such third party as agrees to indemnify the bondsman, the burden of forfeiture will fall on the friend or relative.

As a practical matter, bail is usually furnished by a professional bail bondsman who provides the necessary security in return for a fee. This fee is usually provided by a relative or friend or the defendant himself and may cost between 5 and 10 per cent of the face amount of the bond, depending upon the rate in that area of the United States. If there is a failure to appear, the forfeiture of security takes place. However, some bail bondsmen have been unusually successful in avoiding forfeiture even on nonappearance.

It has frequently been alleged that the bail-bond system is part of an illegal collusion between the criminal community and dishonest public officials. Another problem raised in connection with the underlying theory of the bail-bond business relates to the fact that once the fee is paid, and if no collateral has been left with the bondsman, the only incentives for the appearance of the defendant in court is that he is "honest" or that he is afraid of the bail bondsman. Why then is this system necessary at all, since the defendant should be as "afraid" of the government sanctions as he is of those of the bondsman? Another problem is that, in fact, it is the bondsman, rather than the judge or commissioner, who may be deciding who stays in jail and who gets out. It is the bail bondsman who decides whether the defendant is a good risk, whether the defendant must supply collateral, and, if so, the amount.

Improper Use of Bail

A widely held view is that the bail system is often used to reach improper ends—objectives other than the reappearance of the defendant. It has been reported that some judges are influenced by fear that the defendant will engage in criminal activity if he is temporarily released on bail before trial. Some judges are apprehensive that evidence may be interfered with, and the view has been expressed that "a taste of jail" will do the defendant some good. The degree to which the alleged crime shocks the sensibilities of the community may influence setting of bail. It has also been claimed that bail requirements may be higher against certain minority representatives. In a report to the National Conference on Bond and Criminal Justice of May, 1964, the following conclusion was reached:

> It is plain that, in many Southern communities (and perhaps elsewhere), bail requirements in civil rights cases did much more than merely assure the defendant's appearance in court. In many instances, the net effect of bail demands was to arrest the demonstrators, by exhausting the organization's treasury or temporarily removing the leaders or the participants. Doubtless that consequence was sometimes unintentional, but in other cases, bail was obviously used, even manipulated, to achieve that end. The nature and number of the charges, the amount of the bonds, and the form of security required, in some instances, were plainly intended to delay or prevent release.[2]

The net effect is to punish a defendant before his guilt has been established beyond a reasonable doubt, although this is contrary to basic law.

Appropriate Criteria in Setting Bail

The purpose of bail is to make sure that the defendant appears for trial. In setting bail, the appropriate criteria to be considered are said to be: the nature of the alleged offense, the nature and sufficiency of the evidence, the reputation and character of the defendant, and the financial status of the defendant as it bears on his ability to give bail. It is suggested that the nature of the crime is relevant because the more serious the crime, the more serious the punishment, and hence the more serious the pressure to "jump" bail and flee. What is overlooked in this explanation is that where the crime is more serious, the more serious will be the efforts of the police to find the defendant if he flees. This certainly weakens the argument that the more serious the crime, the higher the bail should be. The same criticism applies to the use of the amount of evidence against the defendant as a factor in fixing bail.

The two factors that do seem to be relevant to establishing the amount of bail are the reputation and character of the defendant, and his financial status as that relates to his ability to raise bail. It is very difficult to evaluate objectively whether any given defendant will appear for trial. However, experience with bail seems to show that defendants who have substantial economic or social involvment in the community are better bail risks than those who do not. The position has been stated as follows:

> If a defendant has lived and worked in the same community for a number of years and is currently employed, if he has a family with whom he lives, and if he belongs to a church, or to a union, or to other social organizations, he would appear to be a good bail risk, almost without regard to the nature of the crime. If, on the other hand, he has no such ties in the city, he would appear a poor bail risk.

The significance of the defendant's financial status is that, if he is stable financially, it is unlikely he would jeopardize that stability, or that of his friends or relatives, by fleeing. It is noteworthy that, in the eyes of the law, bail is deemed excessive if "it is more than necessary to compel appearance."[3]

Alternatives to Bail

Under the law, it is in some jurisdictions permissible for the defendant to leave cash or other assets with the appropriate authori-

ties instead of posting a bond for bail. Once the defendant appears fo
trial, and the matter is disposed of, he gets his assets back, less a sma
service charge. Unfortunately, only the wealthier defendants generall
have the means to use cash bail. But certain judges have resorted t
a practice that helps less affluent defendants to deposit cash. Th
judge may set bail in the alternative, "five hundred dollars, or fift
dollars cash." Thus the defendant may either hire a professional bai
bondsman to post a five-hundred-dollar bond for him, or he ma
deposit fifty dollars with the appropriate official, which sum i
refundable after trial proceedings. This helps the impecunious de
fendant considerably.

Another alternative to bail is parole. In many cases the judg
having authority to set bail also has discretion "to parole the de
fendant, if reasonably satisfied that the defendant will appear whe
wanted." Although a criminal court judge may have authority t
parole a defendant on his own recognizance, the courts have no
been very liberal in using this D.O.R. device. Analysis shows that
where employed, the bias was toward "white collar" offenses an
against robbery and burglary.

SOCIAL IMPLICATIONS OF BAIL

Because the bail system seems to be based on many irrelevant
operative factors, many defendants undoubtedly remain in jail wh
probably could be released with impunity while awaiting trial, i
the bail were set at a low enough figure or if they were paroled on
their own recognizance. Bernard Botein, Presiding Justice of the
Appellate Division, First District, New York Supreme Court, in his
study of bail reform, cites figures that seem to support this contention:

> A 1958 study of bail in New York disclosed that 28% of the de-
> fendants were unable to raise bail in so low an amount as $500, and
> 45% could not raise bail when set at $2,000.
> In St. Louis 79% of the defendants could not raise bail, and the
> same was true in Baltimore and Philadelphia, and 65% in the Dis-
> trict of Columbia District Court. In a survey made of four Federal
> judicial districts, the percentages of the defendants who could not
> raise bail as little as $500 ranged from 11% in one district to as
> much as 78% in another.[4]

The question is important to every tax-paying citizen because of the
high cost of such incarceration. But what is more important are the
costs in terms of human misery.

Justice Botein has put it this way:

> Pretrial detention of defendants unable to post bail has grim consequences—to community and defendants alike. In New York City alone, in 1962, over 58,000 persons, of whom almost 12,000 were adolescents, were confined to prison for an average of one month each, while awaiting disposition of criminal charges pending in city and state courts.
>
> Think of it! The total number of brooding, degenerating days spent in jail by these individuals in 1962 was 1,775,788, with a direct cost to the city of over $10,000,000 for the year. In 1963 Federal inmates spent an estimated 600,000 days in local prisons.
>
> If one adds the money that is spent to support the defendant's dependents who may be forced onto relief rolls and the cost of constructing bigger and better jails to accommodate the increasing detention population, the amount spent by the taxpayers on defendants held in pretrial detention becomes staggering.
>
> But much more significant, in my view, is the price the community pays in human value.
>
> The defendant may lose his job if he is jailed, even if only for a short time. He may be torn by a burning sense of injustice and turned anti-social because of his realization that had he had the means he would have been able to buy his release. Even if he is found innocent, he and his family may be subject to humiliation once he returns to the community.

In addition to the factors mentioned by Justice Botein, there are others, including the fact that imprisonment hinders both the collection of evidence and assembling of witnesses needed for trial and the actual preparation for trial.

Poverty and Bail

Although there has been considerable reform of the abuses of the bail system, it is still generally true today that defendants will be released from jail pending trial only if they can afford it.

> The theoretical equality of the right to bail when all are not financially equal thus has become in reality a deep and wounding social inequality, increasingly oppressive to the poor and the vagrant. It brings to mind Anatole France's ironic epigram that the law in its majestic impartiality forbids the rich and the poor alike to sleep under bridges.[5]

It is important to note that, under the law, the fact that the defendant has limited resources, or is without any resources, does not mean that the bail is excessive. In one case, an impecunious defendant was faced with a five-thousand-dollar bail demand for his release with respect to an indictment alleging the illegal acquisition and sale of marijuana. The defendant sought to be released on his own recognizance, contending, among other things, that his presence was required to enable him to prepare for bail. He appealed from the subsequent conviction. In rejecting the claim that the bail was excessive, the Circuit Court of Appeals ruled:

> The mere financial inability of the defendant to post an amount otherwise meeting the aforesaid standard does not automatically indicate excessiveness. The purpose for bail cannot in all instances be served by only accommodating the defendant's pocketbook and his desire to be free pending possible conviction.[6]

Even where the judge recognizes that an indigent defendant will be penalized, he may feel that he has no other choice but to fix bail that the defendant cannot raise. Judge Luther Youngdahl explained why he had denied a personal bond in one case as follows:

> The most significant considerations which generated the Court's decision to deny personal bond were the defendant's unemployment at the time of the arrest and his general history of unemployment; the defendant's lack of substantial family ties in the community (he is unmarried); the defendant's prior criminal record and juvenile record, which include a number of acts of violence and a failure to discharge the responsibilities and take advantage of the opportunities of probationary supervision of the Juvenile Court; the fact that this nineteen-year-old faced a substantial period of confinement, albeit at the Youth Center; the fact that in the Court's opinion, the evidence weighed very heavily against the defendant; and finally, the absence of any other substantial ties with local community to counterbalance these negative factors.

Judge Youngdahl explained why he felt obligated to condition release only upon a bond for three thousand dollars:

> Although it may appear inconsistent to set a monetary bond for an indigent, it has been the Court's experience that indigent defendants are often in the community on bond, having obtained the means therefor from family or friends. The fact that others in the community have come to the defendant's aid seems to create a new tie or contact with the community which tends to insure the presence of the defendant. The defendant's obligation is then not only to the Court but to those who financed his bond. In this case, if the new tie to the community could be created, and added to the fact that the defendant has always lived in the District and has never been known to jump "bail," plus the always present prospect of apprehension, this would be enough, in the Court's judgment, to justify his release pending appeal with reasonable assurance that he would respond when necessary.[7]

In a very real sense, the defendant remained in jail because he was poor, in spite of the judge's explanation. This distinction between those having financial resources and those who do not may violate the United States Constitution. As Mr. Justice Douglas has pointed out, in relation to the bail system:

> This traditional right to freedom during trial and pending judicial review has to be squared with the possibility that the defendant may flee or hide himself. Bail is the device which we have borrowed to reconcile the conflicting interests. "The purpose of bail is to insure the defendant's appearance and submission to the judgment of the court" . . . It is assumed that the threat of forfeiture of one's goods will be an effective deterrent to the temptation to break the conditions of one's release.
>
> But the theory is based on the presumption that the defendant has property. To continue to demand a substantial bond which the defendant is unable to secure raises considerable problems for the equal administration of the law. We have held that an indigent defendant is denied equal protection of the law if he is denied an appeal on equal terms with other defendants, solely because of his indigence. . . . . Can an indigent be denied freedom, where a wealthy man would not, because he does not happen to have enough property to pledge for his freedom?[8]

Proposals for Bail Reform

The extensive study of and agitation directed to the bail system has resulted in attempted reform. The Manhattan Bail Project was initiated in 1961, to improve the bail system in New York City, by the Vera Foundation, together with the New York University School of Law and the Institute of Judicial Administration.

In this experiment, after his arrest and prior to his initial appearance in court, the prisoner was interviewed, and his past record and the present charge were examined. The accused person was given a certain score in accordance with a weighted point system. If there was no prior conviction, this counted for two points. Job tenure for a year or more, residence at the same place for a year or more—each counted for three points. Verification of background facts was sought, but investigation of the current charge was avoided, so as not to prejudice the accused. After an interview lasting a quarter of an hour, and verification requiring about an hour, the interviewer, a part-time law student, made a determination as to whether the accused was a good risk. If the determination was affirmative, a short report suggesting release on recognizance (R.O.R.) was pre-

pared for submission to the court of arraignment. The judge decide
on the R.O.R. or on bail, after studying the report.

Justice Botein commented on the results of the experiment a
follows:

> At the end of the three year experience of the Manhattan Bail
> Project, 3,505 accused persons had been released on recognizance in
> New York City's Criminal Court. Of these 3,505 persons, 98.6% re-
> turned to court when required. Only 50 persons—1.4%—wilfully
> failed to appear.
>
> This compares favorably with a 3% forfeiture rate in the same
> jurisdiction on bail bonds. Incidentally, the fear that persons released
> on recognizance would go out and commit new crimes is not sub-
> stantiated by the records, which show that only 23 persons—less than
> 1%—were re-arrested on new charges while awaiting trial.
>
> So impressive were the results of the project that in 1964 The
> City of·New York, through its Office of Probation, took over the
> work of the Manhattan Project for the entire city. In the relatively
> short time that the city project has been in operation, over 8,000
> persons have been released on their own recognizance on the basis
> of recommendations, with just about the same rate of "no shows"
> as in the Manhattan Bail Project.[9]

A few years ago, the then Attorney-General, Robert F. Kennedy,
organized·a National Conference on Bail and Criminal Justice. The
conference, attended by four hundred delegates from all over the
country, stimulated bail reform throughout the United States. In
half the states there are approximately sixty projects relating to
pretrial release, operating in all sorts and sizes of communities, including the District of Columbia, Chicago, Syracuse, Tulsa, Denver,
Florida, St. Laurence County and New York City. In some places,
the projects are operated privately; in others, they are operated by
the prosecutor's office, the probation service, the police department,
or the public defender. They employ variations of the Vera approach,
all seeking to supply the judge with whatever information will enable
him to make a decision based upon that knowledge. To this point,
there have not been many cases in which the person released failed
to reappear.

In the federal system, the bail-reform movement ıs also makıng
headway. In 1966, a nearly unanimous Congress enacted the federal
Bail Reform Act, which seeks to assure that defendants "shall not
needlessly be detained" prior to trial in the federal criminal courts.
Because it also applies to the entire range of crimes against person
and property in the District of Columbia, the new statute may become the model for similar reforms of state systems of criminal jus-

ce. Public Law 89-465 marks the first major overhaul of federal bail
w since 1789, when the First Congress adopted the Eighth Amend-
ent, to bar "excessive bail," and passed the Judiciary Act, to confer
right to be "admitted to bail" in noncapital cases.

The Bail Reform Act goes far toward eliminating "bail" from the
ossary of criminal procedure. It encourages release without payment
f money before trial as well as pending appeal. It authorizes a new
ale of "conditions of release," which may be imposed on defend-
its to assure their appearance. It requires judicial officers, in shaping
lease conditions appropriate to risk, to consider the family, employ-
ent, and community ties of the accused, in addition to his criminal
cord and history of appearance or nonappearance at previous trials.
nd, since it imposes severe penalties for failure to appear, criminal
osecutions supplant bail-bond forfeitures as the primary sanction
ainst defendants who flee.[10]

The Act presents serious shortcomings in two major respects: (1)
does not authorize courts to consider the danger to the community
setting conditions of pretrial release in noncapital cases; and (2)
though it subordinates, it fails to eliminate, money as a condition
at can cause the detention of persons unable to raise it.

"The good citizens of the District of Columbia had better take
over," complained federal Judge George L. Hart, Jr. Under the new
deral Bail Reform Act, he had just released eleven criminal defend-
its on nothing more than their promise to show up later for trial.

In time, Washington, D.C., had its first bail-jumping indictment
der the new no-bail setup. On the second day of his trial for rob-
ry and assault, John L. Barringer, twenty-three, saw the tide of
ents turning against him. He then simply vanished. He was arrested
o months later for another robbery, two more counts of assault,
d packing a pistol. Other defendants may well imitate Barringer.
id Assistant United States Attorney Nicholas S. Nunzio: "It won't
ke them long to catch on."

In order to prevent such situations, the law does allow judges to jail
efendants during a court trial. But a judge must set forth in writing
s reasons for believing that the defendant might be likely to flee; the
efendant can then file an appeal to a higher court.

The same rule applies to pretrial release and to the new law's pro-
sion permitting judges to impose the conditions for release, such as
quiring the accused to report to the police daily.

X. Confessions — The Method of Interrogation

THE SUPREME COURT of the United States employed a number of recent cases for a comprehensive reconsideration of the law governing confessions. One of these cases was the appeal of a North Carolina Negro who had escaped from the penitentiary and then murdered a woman in a cemetery.

He had been serving a long prison term for robbing and sexually assaulting another female victim in the very same cemetery. In this appeal, he contended that "he was kept in a tiny cell in the local jail for 16 days, was fed only two cold sandwiches twice a day, was taken to the cemetery during the daytime and nighttime to view the scene of the crime and was forced to walk 14 miles handcuffed in an attempt to break him down regarding his alibi." He claimed further that "he confessed on the 16th day, after a detective, who was also a lay preacher, had prayed over him at a time when his resistance was exhausted." In opposition, the appeal contended that a detective had given the prisoner "peanuts, cigarettes and stuff in addition to the sandwiches." The brief of the Attorney-General of North Carolina denied that there had been any threats or intimidation. "Surely, Davis was not such a sensitive person after all his years in prison that 'cussing' and being called 'nigger' constituted any degree of fear or coercion."[1]

In *Miranda* v. *Arizona,* the Supreme Court, after studying police manuals and texts describing how confessions are best secured, concluded that interrogation, in the isolated setting of a police station, constituted informal compulsion to confess. The majority of the Court also took the position that the need for confessions is overestimated by the police. The minority, on the other hand, felt that a considerable number of guilty defendants would never have been convicted if such a rule had been in effect, voiding, as it does, police practices that had been found constitutional by the Supreme Court only eight years before. Stated most simply, the decision in this case was that no confession may hereafter be obtained for use as evidence without the informed consent of the person being questioned.

The Supreme Court of the United States has made it clear that a confession is invalid if it has been secured by coercion or if the prisoner has been deprived of the right to consult a lawyer. Courts, lawyers, and law-enforcement agencies are quite concerned with the ramification of this doctrine that a confession must be voluntary if it is to be legally used at the time of the trial of the person who made the confession.

Justice Nathan R. Sobel of the New York Supreme Court scoffs at the strong position taken by the police, that confessions are the backbone of effective law enforcement, with his statement that this stand is "carefully nurtured nonsense."[2] District attorneys and police officers usually estimate that from 75 to 85 per cent of the convictions for serious crimes are based on confessions. As an example, former New York City Police Commissioner Michael J. Murphy estimated that in half the homicide cases that were brought to trial in New York in 1964 confessions were essential to the convictions. Yet Justice Sobel writes that a study of one thousand indictments showed that fewer than 10 per cent involved confessions. He adds:

> Confessions do not affect the crime rate by more than one one-hundredth of 1 percent, and they do not affect the clearance [solving] of crime by more than 1 percent.

Justice Sobel's contention is that, in most major crimes, confessions are not important, since "the victim and the perpetrator were known to one another prior to the commission of the crime." He argues that FBI statistics show that 80 per cent of all murders committed occur within the family or other social group.

Professor Yale Kamisar of the University of Michigan Law School and the American Law Institute, goes so far as to suggest that police interrogations should be taped and also filmed. This would enable the judge and the jury to evaluate the emotional condition of the accused at the time the confession was made. At a meeting of public defenders from all over the United States, Professor Kamisar played a tape recording to the interrogation by detectives of a person suspected of murder. The playback was so effective in conveying a picture of the state of mind of the suspect when he was making the confession that the Minnesota Supreme Court set aside the conviction on the grounds that the confession was induced by psychological coercion. It is noteworthy that the accused was later convicted on the evidence that the police already had in its files.

In the Miranda case and other cases decided by the Supreme Court of the United States on June 13, 1966, Chief Justice Earl Warren recited the many instances of resort to physical force or other pressures by police and he condemned them.

VOLUNTARY VERSUS INVOLUNTARY CONFESSIONS

The heart of the argument against the use of an involuntary confession is the guarantee of the Fifth Amendment to the United States Constitution that "no person shall be compelled in any criminal case to be a witness against himself." This privilege against self-incrimination is founded upon the fear of our founding fathers of confessions obtained by rack, thumbscrew, or Star Chamber proceedings. Under this privilege, the accused cannot be compelled to give testimony against himself even at a trial, protected as he is by the safeguards of the common law judicial machinery, and the availability of his lawyer. It is argued that the Fifth Amendment must also protect the citizen at the preliminary stage, the police interrogation, when the accused may feel constrained to make an admission or confession that may convict him at the trial.

Involuntary Confessions

The privilege against self-incrimination forbids the use of a confession in court that has been wrung from the suspect by coercion. What constitutes coercion ranges from physical brutality to veiled threats or even subtly worded promises. But the precise point at which a voluntary confession is deemed to be involuntary is difficult to find.

Chief Justice Joseph Weintraub of the New Jersey Supreme Court has been quoted by the *New York Times* of Dec. 11, 1965, as saying that "there is really no such thing as an entirely voluntary confession." However, he immediately followed up this statement by pointing out that he was not alluding to the type of confession freely given to a policeman by a person who says he truly wants to report a criminal act he has committed. As examples of the latter, Justice Weintraub cited "the husband who calls the police and says he just shot his wife and wants to confess, or the man who walks into a station house and freely offers to tell the police that he committed a crime and cannot live with his conscience."

Mr. Justice Weintraub went on to distinguish the situation from the one in which the "suspect has had his 'will' changed by the police." "No matter how inoffensively, or how gentle the inducement, such confessions are not voluntary even though the courts treat them as such. As soon as we realize this, and stop kidding ourselves, we will stop corrupting the police." He pointed out that, when the policeman who is questioning the suspect tells him that "he'll feel better 'after confession'," in actuality, "we all know that he'll feel worse for it tomorrow."

Mr. Justice Frankfurter of the Supreme Court of the United States enunciated the judicial test of when a confession was considered to be voluntary or not.

A statement to be voluntary need not be volunteered. But if it is the product of sustained pressure by the police it does not issue from a free choice. When a suspect speaks because he is overborne, it is immaterial whether he has been subjected to a physical or mental ordeal. Eventually yielding to questioning under such circumstances is plainly the product of the suction process of interrogation and therefore the reverse of voluntary. We would have to shut our minds to the plain significance of what has transpired to deny that this was a calculated endeavor to secure a confession through the pressure of unrelenting interrogation. The very relentlessness of such interrogation implies that it is better for the prisoner to answer than to persist in refusal of disclosure which is his constitutional right. To turn the detention of an accused into a process of wrenching from him evidence which could not be extorted in open court with its safeguards, is so grave an abuse of the power of arrest as to offend the procedural safeguards of due process.[3]

While there is no absolute test, what the court seeks to do is to balance off the right of the suspect to be free from compulsion in making an incriminating statement against the need of the police to ferret out the facts regarding a crime that may have been committed.

Factors Affecting Voluntariness

Although the judicial rule seems clear and uncomplicated, many difficulties arise in applying this test to a specific set of facts to decide whether the statement is voluntary or not. The Supreme Court of the United States, in an important case, has stated that it would consider the "totality of circumstances."[4] In that case, the court reversed the conviction of a prisoner on the ground that the confession had been coerced. The convicted person was a Negro, with a low intelligence quotient, who had been convicted and sentenced to the death penalty by an Alabama court for burglary and attempted rape of a white woman. Although physical violence by the police was not established, it was shown that the accused had been subjected to questioning, on and off, for nine days.

The majority opinion of the court was that "circumstances of pressure applied against the power of resistance of this petitioner, who cannot be deemed other than weak of will or mind, deprived him of due process of law." Justice Frankfurter wrote, in that case, with considerable insight:

> For myself, I cannot see the difference, with respect to the "voluntariness" of a confession, between the subversion of freedom of will through physical punishment and the sapping of the will appropriately to be inferred from the circumstances of this case.

And just a few years later, in another reversal of a conviction by the courts of Alabama, Chief Justice Earl Warren explicitly stated that "the blood of the accused is not the only hallmark of an unconstitutional inquisition."[5]

As a result of such analyses, the courts are now investigating number of factors before deciding on whether a confession is voluntary. Among these factors are: the duration and extent of the questioning, the use of threats, the status of the suspect, the nature of the coercion, the number of times the accused confessed, the use of special techniques, the past record of the accused, and, of course, the use of physical force.

Duration and Extent of Questioning

The Supreme Court of the United States has held that delay in arraignment was a factor to be considered as one aspect of circumstances in determining the voluntariness of a confession. In one case, a boy of fourteen was charged with the homicide of an old man. Upon his arrest, he admitted the attack immediately. Instead of being released, he was held by the police. Five days later, he signed a written statement in which he confessed once more. During the interval he had seen neither lawyer, nor parents, nor friend. The statement was used in evidence against him at his trial. The Supreme Court reversed, deciding that the confession was involuntary.

The use of extensive questioning has been universally condemned by the courts. The Supreme Court of the United States decided that a confession was involuntary, chiefly because the accused had been questioned by a relay team of law authorities for over thirty-six hours.

Threats

It is clear that when an accused person is threatened with physical violence, and he responds to the threat by confessing, that admission is involuntary in the eyes of the law. However, as time goes on, and the police authorities use more and more subtle techniques, the line between what is a permissible type of interrogation and what a threat becomes harder to delineate.

In one case, the suspect allegedly possessed and sold narcotics. She was told by the police that if she would help the police they would help her to get leniency. They also warned her that, if she did not cooperate, her children would be taken from her and she would be taken off the public-assistance rolls. The United States Supreme Court reversed the conviction, holding such confession improper.

In another case decided by the Supreme Court of the United States, the suspect admitted to the homicide after the chief of police warned the suspect that he would have to bring in his wife. Prior to this warning, the accused had remained silent after he had been arrested as a murder suspect. The trial judge instructed the jury that the validity of the confession was to be decided, in part, on the probable

th or falsity of the confession. The Supreme Court sent the case
ck for a new trial because the instruction was considered erroneous.
e Court criticized the manner in which the accused was questioned.

tus of the Accused

The status of the suspect has been held of some weight in helping
courts decide whether the acts of the police constituted coercion
obtaining a confession. Such factors as previous brushes with the
, physical health, sanity, verbal and written ability, intelligence,
cation level, and youth have also been considered. There is some
dence that race is also a factor.

The Supreme Court rejected an alleged voluntary petition when it
s shown that a cotton picker, who was ignorant and illiterate, had
de his confession after he had been taken into the backwoods at
ht by a number of Texas Rangers, time after time, until he con-
sed.

Likewise, in another case, a twenty-seven-year-old Negro man
I been questioned intermittently until he confessed. He was ignorant
I of low intelligence, having started his studies at school at eight
rs of age and continued until he was sixteen years of age, at which
e he was still in the third grade. The Supreme Court rejected this
de of interrogation, holding the confession to be improper and in-
missable as evidence. It stressed the mentality of the accused in
ching its result.

'n another important case, the Supreme Court rejected as involun-
y the confession of an accused person who had been adjudged in-
e.

The courts have recognized that if an accused is in poor physical
dition, is ill, or is injured, he will be more susceptible to pressures
rted by police officers in their efforts to elicit an admission or
fession from him.

ysical Violence

The most blatant form of coercion is that of physical violence by
police. Federal District Court Judge Jerome Frank once wrote:
'e hear of the merits of the rubber hose; it inflicts severe pain yet
ves no trace." The amount of physical force used by police in
aining confessions is uncertain. But it is undeniable that it has
n resorted to in some cases. And it is also clear that there are
-enforcement agents who are sophisticated enough to use violent
thods that are difficult to prove against them. In their book *Not
ilty,* Jerome and Barbara Frank report the following, from the
moirs of a captain of police:

A sharp, but not heavy blow on the skull, repeated at regular intervals so that the regularity of the blows causes anticipation which would increase the torture; assuring the suspect that he will not be hurt, then felling him with a blow from behind with a club or slab of wood, followed by further sympathy and assurance when the man revives, only to have the same thing happen again, the man never seeing who strikes him.[6]

It is difficult to prove the use of violence or to establish that a confession was involuntary. Police who act in this unlawful manner know enough to avoid battery that will leave bruises or sores for the prisoner's doctor to find. Even bruises heal in a few days, however. And a blow on the back of the head or knees with a rubber hose causes excruciating pain but does not leave a tell-tale mark. Another successful technique is a blow with the fist or with the night stick in the prisoner's stomach.

Other Forms of Coercion and Duress

In another case reviewed by the Supreme Court, the accused charged that he had been abused physically by the police authorities who questioned him. The Court decided this claim against him; however, the Court refused to recognize the confession on the grounds that it resulted from coercion and duress. During the interrogation sessions the prisoner was transported from prison to prison, even though this violated the laws of the state. The Court felt that the confession was not voluntary because of the fears that would be aroused in an ignorant person by moving him, day and night, to new and strange places, interrogating him intermittently, and threatening him with more violence.

Where a prisoner was deprived of food for protracted periods of time, the Supreme Court decided the confession was not voluntary, in the light of the total combination of factors that existed in the case.

Another case considered by the Supreme Court reminds one of Arthur Koestler's *Darkness at Noon*. As soon as the accused was arrested, his clothes were taken from him and he was left naked for three hours. Then he was permitted to put on his shoes, socks, and underwear, and was given a blanket to drape about himself. The District Attorney conceded that the prisoner was kept naked as a technique to make him psychologically vulnerable, to make him fear corporal abuse, and to humiliate him. On these factual grounds the Supreme Court threw out the confession.

Special Techniques

Science is constantly developing new techniques to elicit the "truth." The Supreme Court has recognized that these methods are potentially very dangerous. In one case, the Court held that where a psychiatrist, working for the state, repeatedly interviewed the accused, a fifty-year-old man who was suspected of beating his father and mother to death, such interrogation was not proper. The Court felt that the counseling methods of the doctor made the suspect feel that his purpose was to help the suspect. This "therapy" was considered mental coercion, which vitiated the confession.

The Supreme Court has indicated that the administration of "truth serum" or employing similar techniques may make the confession so obtained involuntary. The test as stated by the Court is:

> If an individual's will was overborne or if his confession was not the project of a rational intellect and free will his confession is inadmissable because coerced. These standards are applicable whether a confession is a product of physical intimidation or psychological pressure and, of course are equally applicable to a drug-induced statement. It is difficult to imagine a situation in which a confession would be less the product of a free will or intellect, less voluntary, than when brought about by a drug having the effect of a "truth serum.[7]

The courts have given some indication that the past criminal record of the prisoner may be taken into account in deciding whether the confession is involuntary. The underlying theory apparently is that if the accused has had a similar experience with the police in the past, he will not yield to coercion or duress as easily as if he has not had such past history.

Quite frequently, the suspect will make an oral confession after interrogation, which serves as a springboard for continued questioning. A number of successive confessions usually follow in which inconsistencies are ironed out and additional details are elicited. It is clear that once the accused has made his first admission, it is difficult for him to recant his guilt, and it is psychologically almost impossible for him then to resume a stance of innocence. The legal question is presented as to whether the final confession, containing statements made in a prior admission or confession that was obtained through duress and coercion, is admissible into evidence. In one case in point, a second confession was made some dozen hours after the first confession had been obtained through coercion. The Supreme Court decided that the second confession was voluntary.

Federal-State Comparison

There seems to be a striking difference between the way FBI agents secure confessions and the manner in which they are obtained by local police in certain jurisdictions. There are rarely any claims of violence or coercion asserted against federal law-enforcement agents. Yet they have a good record of confessions.

In addition to the usual rules and restrictions concerning the admission of confessions into evidence in state courts, the federal courts reject those confessions where the defendant, after arrest, was not brought before a United States Commissioner without unnecessary delay.

Use of Confession

During recent years, the Court has studied procedures assuring that the Fifth and Sixth Amendments were complied with in securing confessions. In *Bruton v. United States*,[8] the Court focused on a different problem—the use at a joint trial of a co-defendants' confession inculpating the other co-defendant. It overruled the rule that such a confession could be admitted at a joint trial so long as the jury was specifically instructed that the co-defendant's confession was admissible only against the declarant.[9]

It made clear that "custodial interrogation"—the key to deciding the applicability of the *Miranda* rule—was to be restrictibly applied. The failure of an Internal Revenue agent to give the Miranda warnings in connection with a "routine" tax investigation required the subsequent reversal of a conviction for tax evasion.[10]

The Court also held that unless the prosecution can establish that the defendant's incriminating testimony at his prior trial was not induced by the admission of a confession later found to have been illegally obtained, his trial testimony cannot be used against him at the retrial.[11]

XI. The Right to Counsel

CHIEF JUSTICE J. EDWARD LUMBARD of the Circuit Court of Appeals, Second Circuit, has called it "highly undesirable to lay down a rule which would deprive the police of the opportunity to question suspects and to use such statements as are found to have been given voluntarily and to have been procured fairly."

Recently, former Attorney-General of the United States, Nicholas de B. Katzenbach, has been even more emphatic:

> It would be ridiculous to state that the overriding purpose of any criminal investigation is to insure equal treatment; obviously, criminal investigation is designed to discover those guilty of crime.[1]

He wrote this in an answer to a letter from David L. Bazelon, Chief Judge of the United States Court of Appeals for the District of Columbia, who had written to the then Attorney-General to criticize proposed changes in criminal procedures affecting arrest, investigation, bail, and other pretrial matters.

Judge Bazelon had asked Mr. Katzenbach to "share [his] misgivings that the procedures discriminate against poor persons and Negroes."

In reply, Katzenbach wrote that the court decisions designed to protect arrested persons had made policemen, prosecutors, and judges "increasingly unjust to the law with respect to arrest and most arrest procedures."

Defendants in low income brackets often face more formidable barriers than bail when they come before the courts. A report prepared by the American Bar Association under a grant from the Ford Foundation showed that at least half of the three hundred thousand persons charged with felonies in state courts each year cannot afford to hire counsel for their own defense.

Efforts to redress imbalances in the scales of justice came to fruition in the 1960's through a series of historic high court decisions and legislative enactments. Prominent among the events that signaled a major revolution in American law was the Supreme Court's *Gideon* decision, followed by such landmarks as the Escobedo and Miranda cases and the enactment of the Bail Reform Act of 1966. The law is clear today that the questioning of a suspect in custody is prohibited unless counsel is present or the suspect expressly waives his right to counsel.

American Law Institute Proposal

Endeavoring to formulate a fair and practical compromise, the renowned American Law Institute has tentatively proposed a draft code of procedure covering prearraignment.[2] Formulated by leading law professors, police authorities, and judges, it provides in substance that when an arrested person arrives at the police station, he must be advised at once that he is entitled to remain silent and that his statements may be used against him. He is entitled to telephone his lawyer, relatives, or friends, and to have access to them when they arrive. This advice and the warning, together with his responses, must be recorded electronically.

A person arrested by a warrant charging a specific crime must be brought immediately before a judge, who will advise him of his rights. A person arrested without a warrant must be advised of his rights by the police. However, the person detained by the police can be questioned at the station house for up to four hours, even without an attorney, if he does not choose to be represented. This interrogation must be taped. After the interrogation, those accused of lesser offenses must be either formally charged or set free.

Under the proposal, where a more serious crime, such as homicide or burglary, is involved, the suspect may be detained for "further screening." This could increase the period of detention and interrogation to twenty-two hours. The suspect is entitled to the assistance of his attorney during "sustained questioning." However, if the suspect does not retain counsel, the police may ask the person detained "whether he wishes to make a statement." If he demurs, the police officer must desist from "persistent questioning." The suspect is either let go free, charged, or released on bail.

In the course of arguing an appeal before the Supreme Court of the United States, a lawyer cited these provisions of the American Law Institute proposals. Justice Hugo Black tartly interjected, "That model code—is that part of the United States Constitution?"

New York Proposals

A new procedure which would do away with questioning, fingerprinting, photographing, and booking a person at a police station, is being actively experience-tested in New York City. The plan, proposed by the Presiding Justice of the Appellate Division of the New York Supreme Court, Bernard Botein, would prohibit the police from interrogating an arrested person except in the presence of a lawyer. The plan contemplates that a person arrested for a felony or a serious misdemeanor would be taken immediately to a place in each county where all the procedures would be centralized. It would also control setting up a twenty-four hour arraignment section of the Criminal Part.

Judge Botein explained that most people who charge that their confessions were procured by coercion or duress claim that this took place in the station house. This would no longer be possible, because, under the proposal, the prisoner would be questioned in court and with a lawyer present. The Mayor and the Police Commissioner have voiced support for this plan.

Escobedo v. Illinois

Just recently, Justice Abe Fortas of the United States Supreme Court likened the recognition of the right to counsel in the police station to the Magna Charta and the Bill of Rights. "It has been the wisdom of the ages," said he, "that some safeguards are necessary, and the Magna Charta and the Bill of Rights were designed to eliminate even the unusual cases of injustice and to lay out a standard for the relationship between the state and the individual."[3] His philosophy was expressed in a colloquy with an assistant district attorney, who said that voluntary confessions are the "highest form of evidence" and that few erroneous convictions resulted from admitting these confessions into evidence. The assistant district attorney then blurted, "Doesn't the community here have the same right under the Constitution?"

The controversy revolves around the guarantee of the Fifth Amendment to the United States Constitution that "no person shall be compelled in any criminal case to be a witness against himself." The principle is so rigid that the accused defendant is not required to take the witness stand against himself even at his trial in court. But what is not so clear are the rights of the accused at the time of interrogation by the police—the preliminary stages when the accused person is pressed to make an admission or confession, which may be used against him at the trial that follows.

Two related cases laid the foundation for the rule that police interrogation is so important to the rights of the accused that, even at this early stage, the accused has the right to stand mute and to the help of counsel; that even a voluntary admission might be inadmissible if he is denied these fundamental rights. In *Gideon* v. *Wainwright*,[4] the right to counsel under the United States Constitution was extended to all state criminal courts. In a later case,[5] the guarantee of the United States Constitution against self-incrimination was also extended to state cases.

In *Escobedo* v. *Illinois*,[6] the Supreme Court of the United States invalidated the confession that laborer Danny Escobedo had voluntarily made, on the grounds that the police officers had neglected to advise him of his constitutional right to stand mute and, also, because they had ignored his request to permit him to consult his attorney, who at that very moment had been in the station house, trying to see him.

On January 20, 1960, at two-thirty A.M., Danny Escobedo was

arrested without a warrant for the murder of his brother-in-law, which had occurred the night before. He was interrogated by the authorities and was released at five P.M., on habeas corpus, having made no statement.

Ten days later, a co-defendant informed the police that Escobedo actually had shot his brother-in-law. The police took Danny into custody and, while they drove down to the station house, the policemen advised him that they had a strong case against him and told him to confess. Escobedo, on the basis of past experience with police officers, simply announced that he wished to consult his attorney.

The attorney for the suspect arrived at the station house between nine-thirty and ten P.M., and sought permission to see Escobedo. This request was denied by the officer at the desk and several other police officers. As late as one A.M., counsel still had not been able to see his client. Meanwhile, the suspect was undergoing a spirited questioning. But he continued to ask to consult with his attorney. He was told that his lawyer did not wish to see him.

Escobedo asserts that, at that time, a police officer who knew the defendant and his family spoke to him alone. The officer allegedly promised him that he would try to secure Escobedo's release if he made a statement involving the co-defendant. Escobedo was confronted by his co-defendant. Escobedo made an oral confession, and, under the guidance of an assistant state's attorney, a written statement was taken. It was conceded that at no point in this entire procedure was Escobedo advised of his right to counsel or to remain silent. The Supreme Court of the United States ruled in that case that the defendant, Escobedo, had been deprived of his constitutional right to counsel. The Court emphasized the "direct relationship" between the importance of the period of interrogation to the police "in their quest for a confession and the criticalness of that stage to the accused in his need for legal advice." Escobedo was questioned in advance of a formal indictment, but the Court felt that this element was not important. It pointed out that, after he had been denied access to his lawyer, the investigation had ceased to be a general investigation of an "unsolved crime." Escobedo had become the accused, and the purpose of the investigation was to "get him" to confess to his guilt, despite his "constitutional right not to do so." It was at this point that the "guiding hand of counsel" was deemed most important for the vindication of his constitutional right.

The Court thus had given up its old position that only when interrogation took place after indictment was there a right to a lawyer. It now held that the interrogation before indictment would be scrutinized, as soon as the police officers shifted from the investigating to the accusatory level and fixed on a specific person.

Miranda v. Arizona

As an aftermath of two years of acrimonious debate, by a number of appeals decided in June of 1966, the Supreme Court of the United States authoritatively answered some of the questions concerning confessions that had been left open.[7] As one rabid libertarian said: "Instead of backing off, the Court has put a full dress suit on Danny Escobedo. All that's left off are the spats and boutonniere."[8]

While the court did not go so far as to outlaw the use of all confessions and, while it did not go so far as absolutely to require a lawyer to be present while a suspect is being interrogated, its decision went far beyond the rule enunciated in the Escobedo case. In general terms, the Supreme Court stated what is now the rule. As soon as the police take a person into custody, they must warn him of his right to stand mute and to have a lawyer at his side. Only if he knowingly, intelligently, and voluntarily waives these rights may they go ahead and question him. If his lawyer shows up, he has the right to be present during the interrogation and to advise his client to say nothing. If he wants a lawyer but cannot pay a fee, the state must pick up the tab.

A number of police departments have been warning suspects, but the method has often been slipshod, and the words mumbled. The warning, at times, has been used as a gambit to establish a relationship with the suspect. The Supreme Court has emphasized that a "heavy burden" rests on the prosecution to prove that the suspect voluntarily confessed, knowing that he could have had a lawyer and could have remained silent.

On June 20, 1966, the Supreme Court announced that the new curbs on interrogation were not retroactive—that they could be invoked only by persons whose trials began after that date. At the same time, the Court also stated that any person who was convicted in violation of the rule laid down in *Escobedo* v. *Illinois,* decided on June 22, 1964, could invoke the rule of that case only if his trial was started after that date.

The impact of these cases will be significant, but exactly how significant, only time can tell. Much will depend upon how the police will carry out the obligation imposed upon them of warning suspects of their rights. The Court has ordered them to be very specific in warning suspects, but it may not turn out that way. If experience is any guide, the lower courts will accept the word of the policeman, usually, rather than that of the suspect, as to whether the suspect gave voluntary consent, and this may have the practical effect of watering down the protection.

Legal Representation for the Indigent

Additional problems are raised by the fact that many defendants are impecunious. There have been few cases decided by the Supreme Court of the United States that have engendered as much interest as *Gideon* v. *Wainwright*.[9] That case upset the conviction of Clarence Gideon, who was convicted of a burglary charge in Florida. The reversal was based on the theory that, as an indigent person, he had a constitutional right to free representation at his trial.

The Gideon case had a special impact in the states of Alabama, Florida, Mississippi, North Carolina, and South Carolina. There, an indigent defendant became entitled to free legal representation not only if conviction could result in the death penalty but in all felonies. In New York, Colorado, Connecticut, and Massachusetts—as well as in Florida, where the Gideon case arose—public defender systems were established, designed to permit law students to defend the poor. In some states—Utah, Idaho, Illinois, Virginia, and New Mexico— legal assistance in felony cases during the preliminary period became available to poor people who asked for such help.

The principle of free counsel for the indigent, as enunciated by the Gideon case, was put to severe tests. An example is what happened in the Watts riot, which took place in 1965 in California. The courts of Los Angeles were deluged with more than four thousand poor Negro defendants. The N.A.A.C.P. Legal Defense claims that these defendants received virtually no legal help. But the California Supreme Court and the Supreme Court of the United States refused to entertain applications based upon the *Gideon* doctrine of the right to representation if requested by criminal defendants.

The Escobedo case left open the question of whether the state had a legal obligation to assign free counsel to poor people.

Just recently, Chief Judge David L. Bazelon of the United States Court of Appeals in Washington conducted a highly publicized exchange of letters with the then Attorney-General Nicholas de B. Katzenbach. Judge Bazelon argued that indigents should be given lawyers at the interrogation stage of a case. Mr. Katzenbach thought not. On June 13, 1966, the Supreme Court of the United States sided with Judge Bazelon.

The law-enforcement officials of many large cities in the United States reacted with consternation. In spite of the institution in some areas of free legal assistance for poor persons accused of crime, it may well be that because of the new requirement, law-enforcement officers will forego the questioning of such suspects, rather than have a free lawyer available twenty-fours a day. Thus, in Los Angeles, persons formerly held were advised that they were entitled to obtain legal advice. They were not informed that free legal counsel would be made available if they demanded a lawyer. If a suspect demanded a lawyer and could not pay for one, the police would simply stop questioning him.

David W. Craig, the Public Safety Director of Pittsburgh, expressed one of the problems involved in providing a free lawyer for the poor.

> If you arrest a person, say, at 11 o'clock at night, and he's indigent, you tell him he's entitled to an attorney from the public defender's office.
> But say you can't get a lawyer until next morning. We're faced with holding him needlessly nine or ten hours and if you do that you're faced with another constitutional question.[10]

The public defender of Pittsburgh, George Loss, voiced his complaint.

> If the police want to question an indigent at 3 o'clock in the morning and the suspect wants a lawyer, the police are going to come to me. Frankly, I don't know what I'm going to do. I can't do it with just six attorneys. I'm not sending a man to the police station at 3 a.m.[11]

Just before June, 1966, decisions of the Supreme Court of the United States in Washington set up a round-the-clock legal referral service for poor persons suspected of perpetrating crimes. It is staffed by lawyers paid for with antipoverty funds and by private volunteer lawyers. It seems likely that this idea will gain acceptance in other cities. Otherwise, the police may have to give up questioning poor suspects who refuse to give up their right to legal assistance during interrogation.

On the basis of past experience, it is possible that the rate of confessions will not go down. Defendants may waive their rights to counsel. In Detroit, Michigan, where the police for the past few years have advised persons held on suspicion of their rights, the number of confessions has not gone down. The figures there show that, in 1965, confessions were given in 58 per cent of the cases. This figure is only 2 percent below the number of confessions made in 1961, when the suspects were not being warned of their rights.

"We have found that restrictions on the use of confessions caused bitter difficulty in advising and prosecuting criminal cases," said Detroit Chief of Detectives Vincent W. Piersante. "Our investigators are aware that confessions are questionable. We now go further to prove a case as conclusively as possible without a confession." [12]

Only time will settle this debate.

Experience Abroad

Even before the Supreme Court of the United States extended the rights of suspects, and contracted the authority of the police, in securing confessions, the solicitude shown suspects during the period of interrogation has been much greater in the United States than elsewhere.

In Italy, suspects are not allowed to have a lawyer while being interrogated, although persons charged with crimes are considered guilty until proven innocent. A magistrate is given six months to carry on an investigation after the suspect has been charged with the crime.

A person is not entitled to a lawyer while being interrogated by the police in France. While such person must be turned over to the magistrate within twenty-four hours, the magistrate may detain him almost indefinitely if he feels that releasing the suspect would jeopardize the investigation. The right to counsel arises only after indictment.

In Japan, suspects must be advised of their rights to stand mute and to be represented. They are allowed to have legal help during the interrogation. However, as a practical matter, few suspects take advantage of this right.

In India, unless the confession is made before a magistrate, it cannot be admitted into evidence. However, the magistrate must advise the suspect that he is not required to make a statement and also that his statements may be used against him. However, attorneys are not available during this questioning.

The same rule applies in England. Yet, the British courts usually do not exclude confessions from evidence if the police have not advised the suspect of his rights. Under the English Judges Rules, which govern arrest and interrogation procedures, the person held may get advice from his lawyer, but only if "no unreasonable delay or hindrance is caused to the process of investigation or the administration of justice."

If a person is unable to pay for a lawyer, he is not provided with counsel in the investigation immediately after arrest. At the initial formal appearance in court, however, a poor person may apply for free legal assistance. This usually takes place the day after the police have finished their questioning. The aid is furnished at the discretion of the judge.

The pressure for change in the United States is chiefly from those who wish to restrict the rights of the police and prosecutors in interrogating suspects. In Britain, there is a growing demand to enlarge the rights of law-enforcement authorities in this regard.

Sir Hartley Shawcross, a highly respected lawyer, has said:

> I think, myself, that suspects ought to be required to answer questions put to them by the police in investigating a crime and in searching for the truth . . .
> I don't believe that there is any kind of ethical foundation for this rule about suspects not being required to incriminate themselves. Why shouldn't they be?[13]

Another outstanding British barrister, Sir John Foster, goes along with this point of view:

> I'd like to see the rule against self-incrimination abolished. That's the same as the Fifth Amendment in America. I'd like it to be said to an accused person—it's your duty to help the police; it's your duty to answer the questions.[14]

In England, where the police are supposed to tell suspects of their rights, it is an open secret that this requirement has usually been evaded in recent years.

A London authority on the law said just recently:

> Let's face it: the English police have been perjuring themselves. They testify to giving the warnings but they really don't. And the judge just winks at it and accepts their testimony.[15]

Lord Shawcross, recognizing the possibility that police may abuse their authority, has proposed that the police put their question to an arrested person in the presence of a magistrate.[16] Such proposals, and others, are the subject of animated and sweeping discussions in the United States and Britain.

XII.

Review of Complaints Against the Police

THE CITIZEN WHO FEELS he has been the victim of improper conduct at the hands of the police has a number of remedies that may be available. He may look to the policeman himself, to his superiors, to the municipality, or to the state for compensation to cover the illegal arrest, search and seizure, detention, or assault. Unfortunately, the person wishing to bring suit for damages is faced with the initial problem of establishing the damages, unless he has been physically injured or his property has actually been taken away or physically damaged. Lawsuits cost money to initiate. Even where the state permits certain suits to be brought, there are many technicalities that make recovery difficult against these defendants. The members of the police department have meager assets available for suit. Moreover, in some jurisidictions, policemen's salaries cannot be made subject to garnishment or attachment.

It is difficult to initiate criminal proceedings against a policeman. The plaintiff may have a criminal record, and this fact will not help his case at the prosecutor's office, which would have to start procedings against one of the "boys," and then be willing to push the case. The criminal case must be proven against the policeman "beyond a reasonable doubt"—no mean task.

Finally, if the citizen only wishes an apology or an explanation, the judicial remedies are really not appropriate. Since the public must protect and encourage the policeman, who has a difficult job, and since at the same time it has an important stake in protecting its citizens from improper police conduct and in weeding out those police officers who are not fulfilling their responsibilities to the community, some other method of procedure is seen to be desirable.

One alternative is an administrative system for handling complaints brought by citizens against the police. There are essentially three types of such systems. Some are administered entirely by the police. Some are for the most part administered by civilians. And some are administered partly by police and partly by civilian authority.

REVIEW CONDUCTED SOLELY BY POLICE

Almost every police department in the country has some system for handling complaints made against its policemen. Generally, these complaints are processed within the department, where they are reviewed and investigated; heard; and penalties imposed, if called for.

Most police departments administer the review of civilian complaints within the department, without outside assistance. Most of these departments do not establish formal requirements for making a complaint. A complaint will be accepted at a local police station or at police headquarters. Usually the complaint may be made in person, by telephone, by letter, or otherwise. A few police departments including the New York City Police Department, have a printed form for the person complaining to fill out and complete. Complaints are frequently made, on behalf of individuals who believe they have been wronged, by civil liberties organizations. Most police departments will even accept oral complaints and follow them up.

Investigation

Very few police departments, perhaps 5 per cent, permit complaints to be settled informally. Most require a regular investigation of all complaints received. The usual investigation entails interviewing the person making the complaint, the witnesses who may be available, and the accused policeman. It may be surprising, but more than one third of the police departments use the polygraph, commonly known as the lie detector. In a California case, the court held that a policeman who refused to submit to a lie detector test was held validly fired.

The investigation of complaints is sometimes carried out at the precinct level, where there is no special unit to investigate the complaints. It preserves the advantage of having someone checking who knows the peculiarities of a certain neighborhood and can use the experience with a given incident to prevent recurrence of the complaint. To avoid the problems that may exist because the investigation is conducted at the local level—namely, the possibility of a coverup—certain administrative safeguards are used. The results and the nature of the investigation at the local level are submitted to the civilian complaint supervisor. He checks the persons interviewed, the questions asked, and the responses. If he is satisfied, he forwards his conclusions to a higher echelon, which determines whether charges should be filed against the policeman. If he is not satisfied, he can direct that certain investigative steps be taken. The investigator must be at least two ranks above the accused officer. A hearing may be convened to assist in ascertaining necessary facts. A method of investigation similar to that used in New York is employed in Los Angeles. The principal difference is that the Internal Affairs Division of the latter city may conduct the investigation independently and on its own initiative. Only a very few police departments have special units within the department to check complaints made by members of the public. The results of the investigations are rarely made available to the persons making the complaints, and in 50 per cent of the cases they are kept confidential.

Hearings

Usually police departments provide for hearings at which the accused policeman and the complaining citizen, as well as witnesses, can appear. Some complaint set-ups, however, do not provide for testimony by the complainant or his witnesses, but only for the appearance of the policeman. Most police departments do provide for an adversary hearing, with both sides entitled to appear. These tribunals are held before boards or they may be heard before a single police officer. Some hearings are closed to the public, but most are open.

Disciplinary Measures

A police officer cannot protect himself against discharge at a hearing by relying on the constitutional privilege against self-incrimination. The courts have clearly decided that a policeman may be fired for refusal to testify under such circumstances.

Usually, if the system of the police department provides for a hearing, the accused officer cannot be deprived of the hearing before he is punished. However, the policeman can waive the hearing and acquiesce in accepting the punishment recommended by his supervisory officer.

Most police department boards can order suspension or censure, but only about half can order that the accused officer be discharged. The board actually may only have the authority to submit recommendations to the head of the department, who in turn makes the final decision. The head will usually adhere to the findings and recommend action proposed by the board.

CIVILIAN PARTICIPATION IN COMPLAINT REVIEW

New York City is in the process of establishing a system of civilian participation in complaint review within the police department. Fulfilling a campaign promise, in July of 1966, Mayor John V. Lindsay named four civilians and three police officers to serve on a revamped complaint review board. The old board was composed only of three deputy police commissioners. Civil rights groups complained that such boards always side with the policeman in a dispute involving a civilian. The make-up of the board became a hot political issue, and Mayor Lindsay, in his campaign, pledged to appoint a civilian-dominated panel in place of the old board. The proposal was killed by the voters, but the department has made changes in order to recognize the civilian viewpoint.

The civilian members of the board are not paid, but are entitled to a fee of fifty dollars for each appearance at a hearing or meeting. It serves only in an advisory capacity to the Police Commissioner. If the Police Commissioner does not go along with the board's recommendations, a departmental trial against the policeman in question may follow, with the trial prosecuted by policemen and judged by other policemen. The Commissioner can also order a departmental trial against a member of the force without a review-board recommendation. A departmental trial's most stringent penalty is dismissal from the force.

Under the former system, the board was administered by police officials; now civilians will handle complaints and, in some situations, administrative work. The old board received complaints only in its offices, while now people can start action by making complaints in person, by mail, or over the phone.

INDEPENDENT CIVILIAN REVIEW

Independent civilian police review boards exist in only two cities in the United States. In 1958, a police review board of this sort was set up in Philadelphia; and, in 1963, such a board was established in Rochester, New York.

The Philadelphia board was set up by the Mayor under his powers under the municipal charter when the City Council refused to approve the ordinance he had initiated for that purpose. It is a genuine civilian board, consisting of eight members and a paid secretary. It is constituted by persons representing a wide spectrum of community interests and opinion. The Philadelphia board has been the subject of litigation and has given rise to acrimonious controversy.

A complaint may be filed by any person, or interested group in behalf of any person, who considers himself the victim of improper police action. The board may either dispose of the complaint informally or may ask the Police Commissioner to investigate. After investigation and consideration, a full-dress hearing may be held. A majority of the Board decides the complaint, and the decision and the penalty, if any, are usually forwarded without opinion to the Commissioner and to the Mayor. If the Commissioner and the board do not agree, the Mayor may step in and arrive at a compromise solution.

It is true that Philadelphia is still not the City of Brotherly Love, but this is not a fair picture of the effectiveness of the system. It has succeeded in bringing citizen judgment to bear upon police affairs and has brought about a new method of informal complaint settlement. However, it has been suggested that the board is hampered in obtaining public confidence by the fact that the police themselves investigate the complaints. Some civil rights leaders feel that the board has been more lenient than the police would have been in some cases.

Norman Frank, the director of community relations for the New York City Patrolmen's Benevolent Association, in arguing on television against an expanded board to review civilian complaints, asserted that the Federal Bureau of Investigation report on the 1964 race riots said in substance that "the existence of a review board in Philadelphia so hampered the work of the police during these riots that they were virtually ineffective."

James Farmer, appearing on the same television program, disagreed. He contends that the riot in Philadelphia was "short-lived," and that at its conclusion there were "no charges of police brutality."

The report of the Federal Bureau of Investigation, of Sept. 26, 1964, said that "where there is an outside civilian review board, the restraint of the police was so great that effective action appeared to be invisible." The report asserted that the police in such cities—which actually were only Philadelphia and Rochester—"were so careful to avoid accusations of improper conduct that they were virtually paralyzed."

Dean Alex Rosen of the New York University Graduate School of Social Work, in a study for the American Jewish Committee of the Philadelphia riot, reported the "calm, efficient police action" in Philadelphia as helping to allay the rioting.

In Rochester, the movement for an independent civilian review board came from clergymen of every denomination, "good government" groups, and various civil rights organizations. The police organization led the opposition to it. Politics played a role in its creation. The board was supported by the Democrats and opposed by the Republicans. Because of the intensity of the feelings displayed in the creation of the board, it has been very conservative in its work.

COMPARISON OF POLICE REVIEW WITH
CIVILIAN REVIEW

There are many general arguments for, and objections to, the various types of reviews, with spokesmen for each position.

Richard W. Welch, Jr., founder and president of the John Birch Society, has written:

> There has been a subtle, but now increasingly bolder and more extensive effort, to harass and discredit local police forces and their individual officials and members going on in our country for more than a decade. The Communist drive to destroy respect for, and the value, strength and morale of our local police forces, has two parallel but separate major purposes.

"Their purposes," Mr. Welch said,

> are Communist-run riots, and attempts by the Communists to replace the local police with their own type of "police" like de Gaulle's barbores or the "federal marshals" used in Mississippi, who bore no community interest or loyalty.[3]

The executive director of the National Police Association has charged that civilian review boards are "one more link in the chain of restrictions which already make our job so difficult." [4]

In response to questions seeking to elicit police reactions to a civilian review board, many policemen said they would turn their backs on minor crimes if such a board were instituted. A number of policemen said they would resign, retire, or transfer to other agencies rather than risk being disciplined by a civilian panel.

"A patrolman who's got a $9,000 job is not going to help you and then get locked up himself. He'll come out and hide for eight hours on the beat. A lot of old-timers now past retirement will get out of the department because of the board."

"We'll have to be extremely careful with minorities," said one policemen. "What if you hear two colored guys arguing and told them to keep quiet and they don't want to. What would you do then? They could find someone to testify against you."

"In this job, you have to make split-second decisions," said a policeman in Brooklyn. "Now we'll have to think about the consequences, too."

On the other hand, Mayor Lindsay has declared that New York needs such a board, and Commissioner Leary has said that a similar board in Philadelphia did not hamper the police.

The Association of the Bar, on April 20, 1965, summed up the problem of the police relationship with the public this way:

Our study has demonstrated that there is no panacea for the problems which underline demands for changes in the present system. We believe that these demands do not really grow out of a movement against the police, but are part of a much larger concern with administrative and enforcement agencies of the government, not only in the United States but also in many other countries having similar systems. There has been, during the past twenty-five years, a large increase in the regulatory and enforcement powers of government arising out of the growth of economic, social and political activities, not the least of which is the growth of population itself. As a result, many people have felt that it has now become necessary to regulate the regulators and police the policemen. In recent years this has been manifested in widespread discussion of the Scandinavian "Ombudsman." In Denmark and Sweden, a somewhat paternal government office has existed for a long time which investigates complaints by individuals of alleged administrative abuses.

Proposals for such an office have been made in the United States at the federal, state and local level. At the recommendation of the New York State Law Revision Commission, there was recently introduced in the State Legislature a bill to establish a Division of Administrative Procedure in the Executive Department to receive complaints from the public and make recommendations on alleged "objectionable agency practices." . . . In Congress, bills have been introduced for several years calling for creation of an "Administrative Counsel" to receive complaints made to Congressmen regarding alleged administrative abuses. . . . In New York City, a recently introduced bill provides for a local ambudsman-type office. . . . The subject is presently under serious consideration in England, Canada, and Australia. An Ombudsman office has already been created in New Zealand.

We say all this to place the issue in its proper perspective; differences between the police and civilians are only part of a larger problem of public administration.[5]

It seems to be a proposal that is worthy of careful study and consideration.

XIII.
Law Enforcement in the Great Society

CRIME IN THE STREETS

AFTER A YEAR and a half of exhaustive investigation, consultations with virtually every outstanding criminologist, and field trips to jails and station houses, the nineteen-member President's Commission on Law Enforcement and Administration of Justice issued its report in June of 1967. In its three-hundred-page tome, the Commission set forth the most comprehensive and detailed analysis of crime in the United States compiled during this century. It hammered home its message of crime in the streets of America with statistics that are hard to ignore. The crime rate has been accelerating at an alarming pace. It jumped 13 per cent in 1964, 5 per cent in 1965, and 11 per cent in 1966. In one year, 1965, there were recorded two and a half million burglaries and significant thefts.

A thought-provoking article by James Q. Wilson, entitled "Crime in the Streets,"[1] which was published in the fall of 1966 in *The Public Interest,* questions the validity of some of the current crime rate statistics. It points out that the crimes that citizens most fear—murder, rape, aggravated assault—make up only a small portion, perhaps 10 per cent, of all "serious" crimes, and that the rates for these crimes have remained fairly constant, have perhaps even declined, during the last few decades.

The apparent increase has been in the "theft" categories. As Wilson suggests, the rise in popularity of theft insurance, inflation in the value of articles of personal property (which in turn converts misdemeanors into serious felonies), the quality and quantity of things left carelessly about in today's affluent society, and the increased use of coin-operated machines have all contributed toward magnifying the theft figures. It has been pointed out elsewhere that the burgeoning crime rate may be nothing more than another expression of the burgeoning gross national product.

Wilson argues that crime-prone groups are no longer encapsulated within certain neighborhoods, but that the members of such groups can now move about through the city with the aid of the automobile. The crimes that were formerly perpetrated within slum neighborhoods and that mostly went unreported are now spilling out over the entire city. Middle-class citizens, faced with crime taking place in their neighborhoods, are quick to panic, quick to call the police.

Certain other statistical factors have not always been considered. It may be that law-enforcement agencies tend to exaggerate the volume of crime (and, as a result, the expansion of law-enforcement facilities is encouraged). It is now established that a majority of assaults and murders takes place among former friends, relatives, and spouses— that is, they are not committed by hardened criminals. Another very striking point was made in a 1965 report entitled *Prevention and Control of Crime and Delinquency,* submitted by the Space-General Corporation to the California Youth and Adult Correction Agency. It concluded that more serious crimes take place every year simply because there are more people every year, and hence more young people, and because there has always been a higher crime rate among young people than among adults.

Thus, despite the actual increase in the number of crimes committed, and an actual increase in the crime rate, there is still no clear and convincing proof that Americans are becoming less honest and more criminal.

But no matter how the figures are analyzed, they are enough to send a chill down one's spine. It is demonstrable that one boy out of six will be hauled into a juvenile court before he reaches the age of eighteen for some offense not related to traffic. Through extensive questionnaires, the President's Commission learned that in certain city neighborhoods, almost 50 per cent of the residents do not venture out of their homes at night, 30 per cent are afraid to talk to strangers, and 20 per cent would like to move out of the areas in which they live. It appears that many citizens are keeping watchdogs as pets; many more people admit that they are keeping guns, for defense, in their homes.

The Commission concedes that even its crime figures are not complete. Much crime, like the proverbial iceberg, is unreported or undetected. It is this submerged portion that is the more terrifying and, perhaps, the most difficult to control. Everyone has heard of assaults, rapes, burglaries, or other crimes of violence, which the victim has not reported because he was embarrassed, or because he was too terrified to complain, or because he did not feel that it would help him to pursue the matter. Obviously, such crimes do not add grist to the statistical mill. Public corruption, tax chiseling, scale-juggling, swindle sheeting are all prevalent in a volume that has not been determined. But even if we go on reported and substantiated crime figures, no matter how the analysis is made, the extent of crime in America is staggering.

The Policeman

The policeman has an important relationship to society and to the rules that make up the fabric of society. But his relationship to law enforcement is not always clearly perceived, either by him or by the public. Today's policeman frequently acquires an attitude of cynicism about his work, his own status, and his importance in the community. He often begins to believe that there are very few people who are concerned about his problems, in the civilian world or even within the municipal hierarchy. He often feels that, if a complaint is lodged against him or if he stands departmental trial, he will lose, or will at least carry some stigma on his professional record, no matter what the outcome. Many policemen believe that it is almost impossible to complete a tour of duty without breaking some police department rule. A member of the force may have a jaded attitude toward a system that seems to call for a quota of issued summonses, and toward the press and the public, who, he feels, regard him negatively or at best with apathy. In spite of the growing number of youngsters going to college, it is interesting to note that, out of each twenty candidates accepted into the New York City police force in the last fifteen years, only one had been to college.

While the police seem to be alienated from the general public, within the force itself there appears to be a greater cohesiveness and group solidarity than ever before. The greater instability in our society today, especially in the cities; the diverse nature of our populations; the general breakdown of respect for authority and established values; all seem to call for greater flexibility and sensitivity from the policeman. Yet the police force today is as authoritative as ever, molded into a conforming, semimilitary caste whose ideas and organization do not vary too greatly from those that obtained at the turn of the century.

But this is only one side of the picture. Citizens do not appreciate the tremendously increasing difficulty of the policeman's job, the subtle judgments relating to social relations and community balance that he must make. Daily, the policeman must exercise his discretion so as to keep things going—so as to keep the powder kegs from exploding. "Crime does not look the same on the street as it does in a legislative chamber," the President's Commission acknowledged. The perilous, violence-laden atmosphere in which the policeman must operate is quite different from the after-the-fact atmosphere of the courtroom. Everyone, the judge, the jury, the lawyers, all have time to deliberate —that is, everyone but the cop. There is no magic formula for dealing with the varied and multifaceted problems that come up on "the beat" every day. No manual can give the precise answers to the conundrums that urban life thrusts at the policeman. "Keeping streets and parks safe is not the same problem as keeping banks secure. The kind of police patrol that will deter boys from street robberies is not likely to deter men with guns from holding up storekeepers."

Laws that make it easy to put guns into the hands of civilians, laws that make it difficult for policemen to use weapons, cause the life of a policeman to be fraught with danger, no matter what the merits of such legislation may be.

The citizen is quite willing to grumble, or even complain more audibly, about the alleged shortcomings of the police. Nevertheless, tradition demands that policemen, regardless of skill or education, start on the beat, at bottom pay, bottom conditions. Thus, it is understandable that it is almost impossible to secure individuals who are skilled enough by training, by experience, and by education, to fill the specialized jobs that the police departments must fill in order to cope with the organized and trained criminals of today.

The President's Commission points out that, in the 212 substantial metropolitan areas within the United States, there are 313 counties and 4,144 cities, each with a separate police department. The Commission makes out a convincing case for combining or coordinating many of these thousands of police forces, so that they may be administered as units in areas with populations of about fifty thousand.

Among the other Commission recommendations are: installation of modern communications equipment capable of maintaining instantaneous communication between policemen in the street and headquarters; use of computerized electronic facilities, to cut down the time between the telephone call for help and the dispersal of the squad car to the place where help is needed; planning of programs for closer relations with the civilian population, which will enable the police to hear community complaints and to present their own objectives and problems to the public.

CRIME IN THE COURTS

Just a few years ago, two outstanding professors of law published what was supposed to be a definitive treatise covering the field of criminal law. One year after its publication, this law school text had to be expanded by an additional two thirds, largely because of decisions of the Supreme Court. In 1967, the Supreme Court dockets were weighed down with a preponderance of appeals in criminal cases, which constituted about a third of all the cases to be reviewed. It is apparent that the professors will soon need a new edition.

During the summer of 1967, Mr. Justice Byron R. White, addressing the Conference of the Chief Justices in Honolulu, reviewed the state of criminal law after the Miranda case[2] gave recognition to the still-unanswered questions in that field.

While pointing out that he had dissented from the majority in *Miranda* and disagreed with the reasoning in that opinion, Mr. Justice White acknowledged that he saw "little difference between Miranda and several other decisions, some old, some new, which have construed the Fifth Amendment in a manner in which it has never been construed before, or, as in the case of Miranda, contrary to previous decisions of the Court and of other Courts as well." He predicted that its main impact would be on the lower courts of the state rather than the federal courts.

In his view, perhaps the most critical of the issues arising from the *Miranda* decision was the question of how to decide whether the accused had actually waived his right to counsel and his right to keep silent. What did the state have to demonstrate in order to establish that the accused had actually waived his right to a lawyer and his right to stand mute and that he had received a proper notification of his rights? Mr. Justice White pondered, aloud, whether the volume of litigation over the voluntariness of confessions would simply be replaced by a like number of cases dealing with the propriety of alleged waivers.

Another issue stemming from the Miranda case concerns the degree to which its newly announced rule excluding certain evidence offered at trial will forbid the introduction of improperly secured statements and evidence compiled from such inadmissible confessions or admissions.

Other cloudy areas are concerned with statements that may not be introduced as direct evidence at the trial of the criminal, but that are offered to contradict the testimony of the accused, or to serve as a basis for indicting him, or to influence other people to testify against him, or to obtain the revocation of a convicted felon's parole, or to influence the judge at the point of sentencing.

When does "custodial interrogation" begin, the Justice asked, in order for the *Miranda* doctrine to be applied? Is the suspect protected only in the police station or is he protected whenever and wherever he is, in effect, restrained by the police? Does the rule attach at any time or only when the suspect is being questioned in a jail after a crime has been committed? To what extent may the *Miranda* rule of right to counsel and warning about confessions be extended to apply to a psychiatric examination, or to the preliminary stages of juvenile court proceedings?

From among recent major decisions in the field of criminal law, Mr. Justice White predicted that several "trouble-makers" would raise significant questions.

In the case of *Warden* v. *Hayden*,[3] the Supreme Court had reconsidered a previously accepted rule and allowed evidence to be admitted where seized in a search incident to an arrest, even though the objects seized were neither the fruits nor the instrumentalities of the crime, but rather were "mere evidence" of the offense (see p. 70). The Justice anticipated that future cases would fill in the outlines of the new approach, making clear what degree of "probable cause" will be needed to authorize a search for "mere evidence," the extent to which valid searches may take place incident to arrest, and the degree of specificity required in a search warrant.

He reminded the Conference that, in *Berger* v. *New York*,[4] the Court declared a New York law dealing with eavesdropping invalid on its face because the law did not require a showing of "probable cause" sufficient to satisfy the Supreme Court. The patent challenge to law-enforcement officials is whether any eavesdropping or wiretapping law can be drawn in such a way as to meet the objections voiced in the Berger case. Commenting on that case, Justice White had observed, "Today's majority does not, in so many words, hold that all wiretapping and eavesdropping are constitutionally impermissible. But, by transparent indirection, it achieves practically the same result by striking down the New York statute and imposing a series of requirements for legalized electronic surveillance that will be almost impossible to satisfy."

On December 18, 1967, in *Katz* v. *United States,* the Supreme Court tried to avoid some of the problems left unresolved in *Berger* by stating clearly that the police may use electronic eavesdropping devices, provided that a warrant be obtained in advance.

In a number of cases, Mr. Justice White pointed out, the Supreme Court had decided that identification of a defendant was not allowed —unless the district attorney has established that the identification in *urt* was made independently—if there had been a pretrial line-up at *nich* the accused, without his counsel, had been identified by the *itness*. The Court, in one ruling, had implied that due process of *w* may be violated in situations where a witness is allowed to view a *ne* suspect in custody before trial and where the circumstances are *ggestive* and conducive to mistaken identification.

Finally, a tremendously important case, which used the *Miranda* *proach*, was *In re Gault*.⁵ This case has opened the door to other *estions*, especially those relating to the juvenile court, since, in the *ault* case, the Supreme Court reserved its opinion concerning the pre- *ninary* and dispositional stages of such proceedings.

dicial or Legislative Rules

In 1937, just three decades ago, the Supreme Court of the United *ates* considered only six cases in the field of criminal law. In 1967, *will* consider six or seven times that many cases. There are a num- *r* of reasons for this proliferation. The number of reported crimes *s* increased substantially during those thirty years. Local judges and *v*-enforcement officials have used their energies mainly to obtain *nvictions* rather than to guarantee accused persons their rights. With *gard* to those rights, there has been considerable diversity among *e* decisions and statutes, which often varied significantly from state *state*. Thus, in New York, the courts would not permit a policeman *break* down the door of a person's house without a warrant; in *io*, this was allowed. In twentieth-century America, where state *es* do little to inhibit crime, this confusing patchwork of laws has *d* a demoralizing effect on judges, policemen, and lawyers, and, in- *lentally*, on those suspect of crimes.

To meet this need, the Supreme Court of the United States, in the *t* few years, began to tick off a set of decisions, which sought to *gulate* police activity in a consistent way throughout all the states. The Supreme Court has been subjected to a barrage of criticism of *e* role it has assumed. Some of its detractors have argued that only *ngress* or the state legislatures should have handled this problem, *ough* legislation. Others have felt that the nature of the Supreme *urt's* criminal-law decisions was such as to "handcuff the police." *one* has suggested that national standardization was not long *erdue*.

Although Justice Byron R. White has dissented vigorously from *eral* of the recent decisions extending the rights of defendants in *minal* cases, he has, at the same time, defended the Court's active *ervention* into criminal administration. At a 1967 conference of *te* supreme court justices, during which many of the justices took a critical view of the United States Supreme Court's recently announced limitation on confessions, Justice White pointed out that both federal and state constitutions were usually drafted in broad language, with the fine points left to be decided by judges. As a result, the high court had the responsibility of deciding questions, such as the confessions issue, one way or another. "I see little reason," he said, "for the judiciary to apologize for doing, as best they can, the very best job which they are bound to do."

A responsible critic of the efforts of the Supreme Court in the field of criminal law has been Judge Henry J. Friendly of the Court of Appeals for the Second Circuit. He has warned that the specification of criminal procedure by the Supreme Court is too inflexible. Since any procedures adopted by the Court must take the form of constitutional decisions, they can be modified only by formal amendment of the United States Constitution or by later Supreme Court decisions changing or setting aside the earlier rulings. Judge Friendly has also voiced criticism of the technical difficulties of implementing some of the rulings.

The Supreme Court decisions, and the attendant lower court cases, have come along so fast, and many of them have enunciated such technical rules, that many lawyers, even those specializing in criminal law, have not been able to assimilate them. The average policeman, who is no lawyer, has to work with an even greater handicap. In the police station, and especially in the street, he may often be frozen into inaction by his uncertainty about appropriate legal behavior. A widespread hue and cry has gone out from lawyers, judges, and law-enforcement officials, who complain that, when handling present problems, they are required to be soothsayers, to be able to predict what law will be announced in the future by the Supreme Court. Many say that they are less interested, today, in the soundness of the criminal procedural rules than concerned with figuring out what the rules are.

The Supreme Court, seeking to prescribe fair criminal procedures, has set forth a number of fairly narrow rules, enunciated in specific cases, detailing what action the police officer is required to take in each situation. If he does not comply with the rule, the suspect, perhaps the perpetrator of a crime, will go free. It has been asked why the Court did not simply formulate a set of broad rules to be incorporated into its Federal Rules of Procedure. Alternatively, it is conceivable that the Court could simply have enunciated a doctrine of fair play in the relationship between the citizen and the police. If a law-enforcement agent took actual advantage of a suspect or actually mistreated him, then and only then would the suspect be freed. But if the policeman made only some minor mistake of law, no miscreant clearly guilty of perpetrating a crime would be allowed to go scot free.

There are some indications that the Supreme Court's attempt to dot the *i*'s and cross the *t*'s of the criminal procedure does not always succeed. Experienced judges, criminal lawyers, and police officials say that some juries are convicting defendants on less evidence than was formerly required.

Many citizens are impatient with legal niceties, feeling that they help the criminals and penalize law-abiding citizens. As Governor Ronald Reagan of California frequently observes, "law and order" is a main concern of Americans today.

BEYOND THE LAW

All in all, the President's Commission on Law Enforcement and Administration of Justice made two hundred concrete recommendations. On the basis of this report, President Johnson and the Congress enacted the Safe Streets and Crime Control Act. With a projected expenditure of almost a third of a billion dollars, it is expected that programs will be developed for crime control and to coordinate all agencies involved in law enforcement, and to encourage the establishment of new police training academies and laboratories. Certainly, these measures should help alleviate some of the problems undercored by the Commission's finding that "America's system of criminal justice is overcrowded and overworked, undermanned and underfinanced, and often misunderstood."

The Commission has stated that one of its objectives "is to eliminate injustices so that the system of criminal justice can win the respect and cooperation of all citizens. Our society must give the police, the courts, and correctional agencies the resources and the mandates to provide fair and dignified treatment for all."

Money alone will not achieve this objective, nor will the law alone bring it to fruition. Judge Charles Breitel of the New York Court of Appeals has put it this way:

> If every policeman, every prosecutor, every court, and every post-sentence agency performed his or her responsibilities in strict accordance with the rules of law, precisely and narrowly laid down, the criminal law would be intolerable.

What is required is the sort of dedication called for by President Johnson in a message to Congress, on March 9, 1966:

> The problems of crime bring us together. Even as we join in common action, we know there can be no instant victory. Ancient evils

do not yield to easy conquest. We cannot limit our efforts to enemies we can see. We must, with equal resolve, seek out new knowledge, new techniques, and new understanding.

POVERTY AND POLICE ADMINISTRATION

Ambassador to the United Nations Arthur J. Goldberg, in an im portant address delivered on October 10, 1967, at Trinity Church in New York, stated:

> Our American constitution distinguishes no social or economic classes and admits of no inequality before the law as between rich and poor. The United States Supreme Court has said that "providing equal justice for the poor and rich, weak and powerful alike . . . is the central aim of our entire judicial system." And a great New York judge, Learned Hand, expressed the same thought in these words: "If we are to keep our democracy, there must be one commandment: Thou shalt not ration justice."

The plight of the impoverished defendant was portrayed by Peter Finley Dunn in the sardonic words of his Mr. Dooley:

> Don't I think a poor man has a chanst in court? Of course he has. He has the same chanst there that he has outside. He has a splendid poor man's chanst.

And, in 1919, Reginald Heber Smith, the father of modern legal aid, wrote:

> The rich and poor do not stand on an equality before the law. The traditional method of providing justice has operated to close the doors of the courts to the poor, and has caused a gross denial of justice in all parts of the country to millions of people.

Former Justice Goldberg pointed up this truth with a number of very practical illustrations.

> All of us who have labored in this field know well how regularly, despite our fine principles and good intentions, both criminal and civil proceedings raise practical obstacles against equal justice for the poor. In criminal cases, a rich suspect may be summoned to the police station; the poor suspect is more often arrested. The rich inebriate may be escorted home by the police; the poor drunk is most often tossed into jail. The rich defendant is released on bail; the poor defendant cannot raise bail and stays behind bars.
> Again, the rich defendant can afford the best legal advice, psychiatrists, expert witnesses, and so on; whereas the poor defendant often

cannot afford to pay a lawyer at all. Instead he must rely upon court-appointed counsel, serving with inadequate fee or often without any fee, and without the resources which are the necessary tools of advocacy.

Then, when the verdict is in, the rich defendant who is pronounced guilty can afford the time and expense of an appeal—a course which the poor man is still hampered in pursuing, despite recent court decisions. If the penalty is a fine, the rich man pays it and goes free; the poor man goes to jail. Finally, the rich man who can be guaranteed a job may qualify for probation or parole; the poor man with no job must more often serve out his sentence.

Alternative steps to shore up some of the foundations of the American legal system began during this decade with a number of epic decisions of the Supreme Court and statutes enacted by Congress. Outstanding in this effort, making what may be a turning point for American democracy, was the decision of the high court in *Gideon* v. *Wainwright*. (For a discussion of this case, see p. 110f.)

During the same period, the building up of social pressures, to a point at which the law was called upon for assistance, focused judicial attention on some of the imbalances that were threatening the quality of life in America.

Legal technicians began to concentrate on the twin problems of urban areas, poverty and discrimination. Increased recognition was given to the real lack of legal protection for the deprived "one third," in matters of both civil and criminal law. Illustrative of this changed awareness is the genesis of neighborhood law offices, available to serve those living in poor areas with respect to such problems as landlord-and-tenant matters, wage claims, garnishees, and the like.

A foment was churned up in the law schools, inspiring many to deeper involvement in the critical issues of American life. Young lawyers were taught the importance of serving in the "firing line" of democracy—the courts—of doing social and legal research, of carrying out projects designed to improve the quality of justice.

In referring to these developments, Ambassador Goldberg observed:

Of course, some people follow a different school of thought and reject this approach as sentimental. In their view the practical, hard-headed answer to crime and violence lies not in the creative force of the law but in its coercive forces: not in more schools and housing but in more prisons.

Against this view, however, we have the testimony of people who are no less practical and hard-headed and who, furthermore, know a great deal about prisons. For example, here are the words of the recently retired director of the Federal Bureau of Prisons.

"There is a hue and cry in the land about violence in the streets and a resurgence of the argument that we must return to harsher methods in which the rights of the individual are subordinated to the lust for retribution and the passion to punish the transgressor. But I am confident that reason will prevail and that our nation will instead try harder to cure the social ills out of which crime and delinquency fester. These efforts will take a good deal of time, energy and money, but they are more likely to bring results. A rich and enlightened nation should at least test their efficacy before returning to primitive and long-discredited punitive techniques."

POLICE-CIVILIAN RELATIONS: PROGNOSIS

One can only speculate as to what impact the restrictive rulings formulated in *Miranda* v. *Arizona* will have on police efficiency, on their ability to catch criminals and see them ensconced in prison after trial. Clearly, the Supreme Court is firmly convinced that certain law-enforcement practices violate basic rights guaranteed to Americans by their Constitution. At the same time, the *Miranda* decision, for all its detail and the prescription of its opinion, does not serve the police as an adequate yardstick to use in determining what is proper in the handling of suspects. A strong case can be made for the adoption of legislative or administrative rules, which the police can follow with some degree of assurance as to what their responsibilities are.

The Court indicated in the Miranda case that its approved method of interrogation could be replaced by statutory or administrative rules. It was emphasized that any such law or regulation would be required to guarantee that a suspect be warned of his right to counsel and to stand mute, and also that he be given a chance to exercise these rights. The Supreme Court, of course, always has the ultimate check on the police. Nevertheless, administrators, legislators, and the police, themselves, can avoid court dictation by promulgating and employing policies that realistically meet the needs of efficient law enforcement and, at the same time, protect the individual.

The report of the President's Commission on Law Enforcement and Administration of Justice has stated it well:

If the present trend continues, it is quite likely that some current investigative practices and procedures thought by the police to be proper and effective will be held to be unconstitutional or subjected to restrictive rules. Whether this happens will depend in some measure upon whether the police, first, can develop policies that differentiate the proper from the improper investigative practices, and whether, second, they can insure through proper supervision that individual officers are held to these policies. In an equally large measure, State legislatures are responsible for establishing police policy.

And, not too long ago, *The New Republic* summed up the issue:

The community acting through its elected representatives must decide and state precisely what it wants the police to do, not simply admonishing them for disobeying indistinct or nonexistent commands.

XIV.

Police on the Campus

THE REPORT OF THE COMMISSION on Campus Unrest appointed b
President Nixon, urged him, in the fall of 1970, with the reopenin,
of schools, to try to bridge the gap between the established societ
and the new youth culture.[1] The commission unanimously warne
that unless that gap could be closed, America could disintegrate int
near civil war—"a brutal war of each against all."

In powerful, very moving terms, the commission condemned witl
impatient conviction fanatical student terrorists, phlegmatic campu
administrators, brutal police officials, punitive action, and incitin
language of political persons. Its report suggested dozens of very
concrete proposals to colleges, police agencies and the governmen
for avoiding or ameliorating campus disorder.

This Scranton commission was appointed by President Nixon
ninety days before its report, following the killing of students by
national guardsmen at Kent State University and by law enforcement
officers at Jackson State College in Mississippi. Its mission was to
investigate the cause and to propose possible solutions for the disorders that had affected hundreds of campuses.[2]

The commission said that peaceful dissent must be defended, and
encouraged, but asserted, "We utterly condemn violence. We especially condemn bombing and political terrorism." It went on:

"Students who bomb and burn are criminals. Police and national
guardsmen who needlessly shoot or assault students are criminals.
All who applaud these criminal acts share in their evil."

In the law enforcement sector, the commission sharply assailed
the use of rifles and bayonets on campus: "Sending civil authorities
onto a college campus armed as if for war—armed only to kill—has

brought tragedy in the past. If this practice is not changed, tragedy will come again."

The report called for providing nonlethal weapons like tear gas to national guardsmen and for rules to insure that deadly force was not used except "as the absolute last resort."

Specifically in the field of law enforcement, it reported:

> We have deep sympathy for peace officers—local and state police, national guardsmen and campus security officers—who must deal with all types of campus disorder. Much depends on their judgments, courage and professionalism.
>
> We commend those thousands of law enforcement officers who have endured taunts and assaults without reacting violently, and whose careful conduct has prevented violence and saved lives.
>
> At the same time, we recognize that there have been dangerous and sometimes fatal instances of unnecessary harshness and illegal violence by law enforcement officers.
>
> We therefore urge that peace officers be trained and equipped to deal with campus disorders, firmly, justly and humanely. They must avoid both uncontrolled and excessive response.
>
> Too frequently, local police forces have been undermanned, improperly equipped, poorly trained and unprepared for campus disturbances. We therefore urge police forces, especially those in smaller communities, to improve their capacity to respond to civil disorders.
>
> We recommend the development of joint contingency plans among law enforcement agencies. They should specify which law enforcement official is to be in command when several forces are operating together.
>
> Sending civil authorities to a college campus armed as if for war—armed only to kill—has brought tragedy in the past. If this practice is not changed, tragedy will come again. Shoulder weapons (except for tear gas launchers) are very rarely needed on the college campus; they should not be used except as emergency equipment in the face of sniper fire or armed resistance justifying them.
>
> We recommend that national guardsmen receive much more training in controlling civil disturbances. During the last three years, the Guard has played almost no role in Southeast Asia but has been called to intervene in civil disorders at home more than 20 times.
>
> We urge that the National Guard be issued special protection equipment appropriate for use in controlling civil disorders. We urge that it have sufficient tactical capability and nonlethal weaponry so that it will use deadly force as the absolute last resort.

The President's Commission on Campus Unrest criticized law enforcement officials in two special reports dealing with Kent State University and Jackson State College shootings. The reports blamed "overreaction" by the National Guard for the killing of four students at Kent State, and characterized the fatal shooting of two students at Jackson by Mississippi state police as the direct result of a "black-white" crisis.

The commission labelled the killing of the six students as "completely unjustified." Joseph Rhodes, Jr., said that the commission discovered "a remarkable, incredible lack of concern for the human life of black people" among the police in Jackson. He said that the commission found at both Kent and Jackson, "the use of deadly force that was used was completely unjustified."

Demonstrations and Free Speech

Every day newspapers set forth the details of some sort of demonstration, some take place on campus, some do not. These demonstrations take a variety of forms and seek to further a variety of causes. There have been sit-ins, teach-ins, be-ins, and even swim-ins. The causes have been related to women's liberation, labor disputes, but have also concerned civil rights, the draft, Vietnam or Cambodia, disarmament, Apartheid, school administration, and calls for hot lunches for children. The police are challenged to decide how far the state or federal or municipal government can go in maintaining "law and order" without invading freedom of expression.

Demonstrations present problems which may accompany free speech. Overt conduct which accompanies the speech may be more conducive to violence or public disorder than speech alone.

R. Harcourt Dodds, Deputy Commissioner for Legal Matters of the New York City Police Department, stated in a talk to the City Club of New York:[3]

> An officer on the street is constantly faced with the problem of deciding what action to take when the conduct of demonstrators gets into the "grey" area. He must determine when legal boundaries are in danger of being exceeded. He must try to admonish tactfully those responsible, while not giving the impression that he is obstructing their legitimate efforts. He must decide when the exercise of a legal right ends and a trespass begins. He must know at what point a previously peaceful group becomes disorderly, when it obstructs vehicular and pedestrial traffic or otherwise interferes with the rights of others, and when positive police action is required. He is the cynosure of all during these times. Experience teaches us that whatever his decision and subsequent action, there will be criticism and resentment from one quarter or another.

The Supreme Court of the United States has recognized this difference. In Cox v. Louisiana, it has said:[4]

> We emphatically reject the notion urged by appellant that the First and Fourteenth Amendments afford the same kind of freedom to those who would communicate ideas by conduct such as patrolling, marching and picketing on streets and highways, as these amendments afford to those who communicate ideas by pure speech.

Police officials, because of their work, sometimes feel that the free expression of ideas by demonstrations often brings in its wake violence, intimidation and, as a matter of fact, interference with free speech.

The director of the Third Division of the New York City Police Department, which covers most of mid-Manhattan, puts it this way:

> Any time you have a crowd, you have to be prepared for certain eventualities—obstruction of movement, panic, violence, etc.
> . . . Crowds are much easier to handle when mobile. An obstruction is always a source of trouble because it, more than unpopular speech or demonstrations for unpopular causes, can lead to short tempers and violence.
> . . . Many civilians will come up to the police and demand to know why certain people are arrested. In some neighborhoods, people may be more resentful than in others. . . . Some people are resentful of nonconformist dress and appearance. . . . In general we plan ahead to police the viewers as well as the demonstrators, making use of whatever information we may have about each.[5]

The various types of disorder which have been considered sufficient to justify restriction of the right to demonstrate include violence, obstruction of traffic, intimidation of courts, picketing for an unlawful purpose, and extreme noise.

The law is clear: the demonstration loses its protection under the Constitution when it is the cause of substantial disorder. However, even when there is no actual disorder, the protection may be lost because of the existence of a "clear and present danger" of a breach of the peace.

There is only one case,[6] in which the Supreme Court applied the "clear and present danger" test to sustain a conviction resulting from a demonstration where there had been no actual violence. In that case, about seventy-five or eighty people, both black and white, had gotten together on a street corner in Syracuse, New York. The defendant, a man named Feiner, had apparently been urging blacks to rise up in arms and fight for equal rights. These words of "incitement to riot" caused the restless gathering to become more excited and to press about Feiner. One person in the crowd threatened violence if the two policemen who were there "did not act." Feiner refused to desist, although there were three police requests that he do so. He was arrested and later convicted of disorderly conduct. The Supreme Court affirmed the conviction and applied the test of "clear and present danger" concluding:

> The findings of the New York courts as to the condition of the crowd and the refusal of the petitioner to obey the police requests . . . are persuasive that the conviction of the petitioner for violation

of public peace, order and authority does not exceed the balance of proper state police action.

In a number of recent demonstration cases the Court has seemed quite reluctant to find the existence of a clear and present danger. Edwards v. South Carolina,[7] concerned the convictions of about 190 demonstrators who marched on to the state house grounds at Columbia, South Carolina, for the purpose of protesting racial segregation. There were thirty or more police officers present and about 300 spectators, including some 11 "possible troublemakers." There were no hostile remarks, no obstruction of traffic, no actual violence or threat of violence by the demonstrators. The demonstrators clapped their hands, stamped their feet, sang songs and listened to a "religious harangue" by one of their leaders. When the demonstrators refused to obey the order of the city manager to march on and disperse, they were arrested. The Supreme Court reversed the convictions.

In a later case, Cox v. Louisiana,[8] about two thousand people got together in front of the state courthouse where several demonstrators who had been arrested the day before were in jail. The demonstrators were five feet deep, but they did not obstruct the street, even though they occupied almost the entire block. They waved signs and sang songs, which brought about a response from their colleagues in the courthouse jail. Cox spoke to the group and concluded with a plea to "sit-in" at uptown lunch counters. The sheriff construed this as being inflammatory and ordered the group to disperse. They refused, and the sheriff finally resorted to the use of tear gas. Cox was arrested the next day and was convicted of disturbing the peace, obstructing public pastures, and courthouse picketing. The Supreme Court again set aside these convictions and described the case as "a far cry from the situation in Feiner v. New York."

A comparison of the Feiner case with the cases of Edwards and Cox seems to make it plain that a "clear and present danger" or disorder will be found only in those instances where there is a combination of inadequate police protection, words of incitement from demonstrators, threats of disorder from spectators, and obstruction of free passage. The omission of one or more of these elements may mean that the situation cannot be considered to constitute a "clear and present danger."

There are three available methods by which the state can maintain orderly demonstrations. The first is to punish unlawful acts by the demonstrators through the use of the various provisions of the criminal law. Another is to have a licensing ordinance which requires a permit in advance of the demonstration. The third is to apply to the courts in an appropriate situation for an injunction regulating the conduct of the demonstrators. The line between insurrection and legitimate expression is a nettlesome one. This can be seen in the case of William Epton who shouted "we will not be fully free until we smash the state completely and totally," to the crowd gathered on the first evening of the riots which took place in the streets of Harlem in 1964. A short while later that same night Epton advised, "In that process, we're going to have to kill a lot of these cops, a lot of these judges, and we'll have to go up against their army." Epton, who had left the Communist party because he felt it restricted him too much in advancing his ideas, was convicted in New York of conspiring to riot and advancing and conspiring to advocate criminal anarchy. He appealed his conviction and his one year concurrent sentence to the Supreme Court of the United States.[9]

It was anticipated that the Court would use this case as a pulpit from which to tell how far demonstrators and their leaders can go before the First Amendment guarantee of free speech yields to the necessity of protecting the public from riots and rampage. However, the Court ignored this chance and dismissed Epton's appeal with an unsigned order. As more and more groups resort to demonstrations to forcefully indicate their views and to influence the government and private groups, the dilemma of balancing the public interests in both keeping order and preserving free speech becomes more difficult and more painful.

Action as Symbolic Speech

In the name of the "Poor People's Campaign," an indignant band of youngsters blew off steam by hurling rocks through the windows of the Supreme Court. Was this act a crime or was it "symbolic speech," protected by the First Amendment?

The Supreme Court has cast the protective mantle of free speech over such acts as flying of a red banner, the carrying of placards by union pickets, the salute of the American flag, and sit-ins in a public library. However, former Chief Justice Warren sought to limit the extent to which action can be regarded as symbolic speech. He once wrote, "We cannot accept the view that an apparently limitless variety of conduct can be labeled 'speech' whenever the person engaging in the conduct intends thereby to express an idea."

The case[10] in which this view was expressed began on a chilly day in March, 1966, when four youths ignited their draft cards with a cigarette lighter on the steps of the south Boston Courthouse. These acts had been well advertised in advance; so well, in fact, that the boys were apprehended by waiting FBI agents. The youths were arrested and convicted, for not carrying their draft card as required by the Selective Service Act of 1948. One of the young men, David P. O'Brien, appealed his conviction. However, in a seven-to-one decision, the Supreme Court upheld the Congressional Act by comparing the burning of draft cards to the destruction of tax records.

Justice Warren, groping to find a more precise definition of symbolic speech, wrote that acts of dissent can be punished if the government has "an important or substantial and constitutional interest in forbidding them, if the incidental restriction on expression is no greater than necessary, and if the government's real interest is not to squelch dissent."

Demonstration Guidelines

Although this has been a decade for demonstrations, the rules governing them are not clear to most Americans. This is not strange. The First Amendment to the Constitution already promises to everyone the right to speak freely and to assemble peaceably for the purpose of petitioning public officials for redress of grievances. However, there is no right under the Constitution to voice dessent in any place at any time. Public officials have the authority to restrain public speech or acts which clearly threaten to inspire violence or interfere with some other valid right of society.

There are various law, judicial decisions or practices in different areas asking for local variations in the rules regulating the conduct of demonstrations. Some may be violative of the Constitution but have so far not been declared by the courts as such. Thus, the Supreme Court has not as yet decided the constitutionality of the 1968 laws of Congress which imposes a five-year jail term or $10,000 fine for crossing a state boundary to instigate or participate in a demonstration which may become violent, even though it may never come to pass. As another example, in Athens, Georgia, white demonstrators can get parade permits in six hours while black people have to wait six months. In several states, including South Carolina, anyone who hangs the flag wrong side up may be sent to jail. Yet, Pennsylvania allows the flag to be desecrated as a permissible form of political expression.

Gradually, a pattern is emerging from the decided cases which spell out the rules of demonstrations which apply to hardhats and longhairs. Among the more settled rules are the following:

Street Speeches: Public speeches espousing political or religious causes do not require permits, even if the expression of such ideas is likely to cause a crowd to collect. A New York City ordinance requires speakers to exhibit an American flag, though this is not enforced too strenuously. The general rule governing street-corner speeches is that powerful verbiage is allowed, but inflammatory rhetoric that may result in violence is not permitted. The courts are having a difficult time in drawing the line between the two.

Distributing Leaflets: The distribution of leaflets is not treated as littering if it is done in public streets for the purpose of advocating political or social causes. However, those receiving the flyers may be fined or arrested if they litter the streets with the "throwaways."

Sidewalk Demonstrations: Marches and picketing on the sidewalk generally cannot be stopped by officials. However, a number of municipalities require permits. In Illinois, picketing in front of private dwellings is not permitted. The protection for such demonstrations probably extends to marchers in privately owned ways provided that such thoroughfares, such as shopping arcades and parking lots, are used on a regular basis by the public.

Provided they are peaceful, demonstrators can march as much as they wish. They can stretch out their line of march and chant or sing. They may even cause minor inconvenience to passersby without penalty, provided such consequences are simply incidental to the main purpose.

Unless the police officers have reason to believe that the demonstrators are stopping traffic or normal pedestrian movement, pickets who remain stationary instead of marching may not be arrested for failure to heed the request of the policemen to keep moving.

Parades on Streets: Almost everywhere, the employment of sound equipment, demonstrations in parks, and street parades require permits. While standards for the issuance of such permits vary, permission may not legally be refused on an arbitrary basis. As an aftermath to the riots which occured during the 1968 Democratic Convention, Chicago passed a new ordinance compelling the city to issue permits within two days after applications are filed. Out of its practical experience, the New York Civil Liberties Union advises: "It may be well to apply for such a permit. If you don't get it, you will then have a better defense if you are arrested."

Arrest of Demonstrators: The law is clear that once a person is taken into custody, police may not interrogate him until they inform him of his rights to stand mute and of his right to an attorney. However, even if the arrest is improper for some reason, the act of laying down or remaining limp, may be treated as a separate charge of resisting arrest. Third parties may be accused of interfering just because they have been standing around. Since a witness who is arrested is not very persuasive, attorneys recommend that witnesses who believe that the police have acted improperly should remain quiet and remember or jot down facts such as the policeman's shield number.

It is proper for the officer to search demonstrators before or after an arrest if they have reasonable cause to believe that they are carrying concealed weapons. Again, the New York Civil Liberties Union, pragmatically advises: "If the police tell you to move, ask them where to and try to go there."

XV.
Police in the Ghetto

GUERILLA WARFARE IN THE STREETS

ACROSS THE MAP of America, in such widely disbursed places as Bedford-Stuyvesant, Watts, Harlem, South Side, Hough, Dixie Hills, Hunters Point, are deployed the thin blue lines of policemen. Their mission is to maintain peace and order. They often feel as if they belonged to an army of occupation; and they are often so regarded by the denizens of those localities. The police stations are line garrisons of a foreign legion, too often an outpost surrounded by destruction and death, despair and desperation. In many places, quiet seems like a lull before a storm, rather than the domestic tranquility which the preamble to the United States Constitution sets forth as a national objective.

Two incidents point up dramatically the tragic state of affairs which exists in America as the seventies begin. Thirty members of the fifty-four man police department in a quiet New Jersey community have, on their own, put together a riot squad. It is equipped with rifles, bayonets, and even an army vehicle. The group holds itself out as available to nearby towns for riot duty. There are no riots in their own peaceful residential community.

In Philadelphia, a worker for the United States Census complained of the difficulty of gathering information about the black population because many of the ghetto dwellers have the idea that the data is being collected as a step in a plan to exterminate the black people.

This crisis has been brewing for a long time but its pace has accelerated in the last ten years. The warnings have been loud and clear. They have been manifest in the explosions of ghetto violence. Many, many, studies, including those of presidential commissions, have underscored the growing division between races, and it is

143

difficult to ignore the growing violence, as well as the desperation of the statements by militant racial leaders and the pessimism of black moderates.

While the summer of 1970 did not see the widespread ghetto rioting which took place in the last years of the last decade, there were an increasing number of incidents in which policemen were attacked, guerilla-style. In July, a white policeman was shot and killed as he sat in his patrol car writing a report, on the South Side of Chicago. A month later, seven policemen were wounded and one killed by a bomb blast in Omaha. The officers were checking on a report that a woman was "screaming." Another policeman had a bullet crease his skull just as he heard, "You're a dead mother_____!" in an almost all black neighborhood of Los Angeles. Practically each day the newspapers tell about another incident to add to this list.

The pace of these deadly and horrifying assaults has changed geometrically. In addition, another element seems to be emerging. The black extremists are adopting traditional guerilla tactics to urban warfare. In Illinois, a state trooper was wounded by a sniper while he was patrolling a predominantly black housing project. A bomb exploded in a patrol car as two police officers were investigating a burglary report in San Francisco. Four policemen were shotgunned in what appeared to be an ambush by Mexican-Americans in California. A policeman investigating a report of gunfire in a Brooklyn, New York, boat club was wounded in his right arm by a sniper's bullet; and he was the fourth New York City policeman to be the victim of a would-be assassin in less than a week. In spite of assiduous efforts, the police could not even turn up a suspect.

In Philadelphia, within three days, one officer was shot dead and six others were wounded. The deceased policeman was sitting quietly behind his desk when the gunman walked up to him in the station house and pumped five shells into him. Every policeman on foot or in a patrol car has to worry about a sniper's bullet or an assassin's knife. He has to sweat it out each time he passes a shadowed alley or darkened window. By late summer 1970, an unprecedented number of policemen had been killed in unprovoked attacks. It was more than double the F.B.I. figure for all of 1969, and nearly four times the national average for each of the past ten years. In 1969, there was an all-time high of eighty-six deaths in the line of duty; 1970 threatened to see that figure exceeded.

The Black Grievances

Is the distrust of the police by blacks really warranted? Patrick V. Murphy, who left Detroit to become the Police Commissioner of the City of New York, faced up to this question:

"Historically, it certainly is warranted," he explained. "When police dogs were used on people by police in the South, every policeman in the country suffered the next day as a result. Here in Detroit a constant complaint of black people is that we don't give them enough service. Black people often feel that we don't respond to their calls as rapidly as we would to a call in a white neighborhood."

A study of black attitudes in Harlem and Watts indicates that ghetto residents are more concerned about their need for police protection than about their other grievances. The survey revealed much hostility among blacks toward the police. It also showed that many blacks sympathized with the problems of the police. They wanted more, instead of fewer, policemen in their neighborhoods.[1]

In September of 1970, a government study[2] substantiated the need for more police in the ghettos. It concluded that the rate of violent crime by urban blacks appears to be markedly higher than for whites —and that blacks also, it added, constituted the majority of the victims. The report, a 2,436-page document, stated that urban blacks are arrested eight to twenty times more often than whites for homocide, rape, aggravated assault and robbery.

The study also reported that except for robbery, sixty to seventy percent of the victims are black. Despite widely held fears by whites, it found "one of the most striking and relevant general conclusions" to be that violent crime is predominantly intraracial.

"The urgent need to reduce violent crimes among urban Negro youth is obvious," it read, "requiring a total effort toward changing the demoralizing conditions and life patterns of Negroes, the unequal opportunity and discrimination they confront . . . and the overcrowding and decay of urban ghettos."

This report, dealing with individual acts of violence, is one of seven submitted to the National Commission on Causes and Prevention of Violence. Lloyd N. Cutler, executive director of the commission, commented: "We have been concerned that some people would fail to recognize that crime is inherent among young slum residents, regardless of race, and see only 'black crime' merely because slums are now largely black."

The report said that, for the population as a whole, persons 18 to 24 commit almost four times as many violent crimes as do persons over 25. "To be young, poor, male, and Negro, to want what the open society claims is available, but mostly to others; to see illegitimate and often violent methods of obtaining material success; and to observe others using these means successfully and with impunity, is to be burdened with an enormous set of influences that pull many toward crime and delinquency."

In spite of the recognition by ghetto dwellers of their need for protection and their dependence upon police, much hatred for the system simmers in the black community. "The seeds of hatred and violence have been sown for a long time now," said Police Chief Bruce R. Baker of Berkeley, California. "The harvest is finally being reaped."

James Riordan, Chief of the patrol division for the Chicago police, has said: "People believe that an attack on policemen is really an attack on society. It's the symbol of authority that's being attacked." Clarence Coster of the Justice Department's Law Enforcement Assistance Administration agrees: "It's this whole confrontation with the establishment; and the policeman is the most visible part of that establishment."

However, the animus of the blacks toward the police is not simply based upon unconscious or subconscious emotional factors. There are genuine grievances which embitter and infuriate the blacks. One of these complaints is depersonalized and brutal treatment. Just after the police deaths in Philadelphia, the police raided three Black Panther headquarters. At one of them, the officers forced the captives to strip naked on the public street for a search.

There is no accurate count of how many blacks, Puerto Ricans or Mexican-Americans have been bullied by the police under ambiguous circumstances or without valid reason. For instance, the President's Commission on Campus Unrest accused Mississippi policemen of "unreasonable, unjustified overreaction," when they fired shotguns, machine guns, rifle and armor-piercing shells into a crowd of black students at Jackson State College in May of 1970.[3] Two blacks were killed and twelve were injured.

The tally would include six blacks shot in the back during riots in Augusta, Georgia; two Mexicans killed in Los Angeles when police burst into an apartment looking for a suspect who wasn't even there; and a black student slain in Lawrence, Kansas. This last death was given scant attention until a white student was slain a few days later.

In late 1970, the Los Angeles police charged into the edges of a crowd which had convened for an anti-war demonstration in the Mexican-American barrio. During the melee which ensued, two men were killed. One of them was Ruben Salazar, a well-known and established television and newspaper commentator for the *Los Angeles Times*. He was killed when a policeman fired a powerful tear-gas projectile (designed for piercing barricades) into a nearby barroom and shattered his head.

Many police officials are convinced that there is a planned and deliberate terrorism by the black community. Others dispute the conspiracy theory. Plot or not, experienced law enforcement experts feel that there is a climate of violence which is endemic. Many of the incidents and guerilla-style attacks on policemen by blacks have been laid at the door of the Black Panthers. An experienced police official has explained their influence this way: "This isn't a case of some Panther big shot telling the party chapters that the time has come to go after the cops. There is no overall coordination of the shootings. There isn't any doubt, though, that the sniping is the direct result of the Panther's 'off the pigs' propaganda. The Panthers, with all their talk of killing policemen, have escalated violence. It's beginning to build into warfare."

The president of the New York Patrolman's Benevolent Association, Edward Kiernan, evaluates these attacks as a manifestation "of a cold, logical, hard-eyed revolutionary strategy." Police Chief Bruce Baker reasons that a black militant reads about attacks on the police in the newspapers or sees it on television, and figures: "I'd better get in on this." Dr. John Spiegel, head of the Lemberg Center for the Study of Violence at Brandeis University, takes a position which bridges the conspiracy theory and the view that the attacks are isolated and unplanned. He explains that an attack in one city can set off a contagion which will spread elsewhere.

This view is accepted by John Lacoste, deputy chief of police in Emeryville, California. He offers the view that such contagion is not restricted to the black community in its stimulation. "If a group like the Weathermen create an atmosphere of tension and hate, it is much easier for a black man who has possibly been abused or thinks he has been abused—to go ahead and 'execute' a policeman, especially where other black groups advocate these 'executions.'"

In Philadelphia, the black rector of the Episcopal Church of the Advocate who enjoys a good relationship with many militants, describes the assaults on the police as a "kind of Sampson syndrome," especially on the part of young people who express their feelings of frustration and inadequacy by lashing back blindly. A Harris poll showed that while fewer older people agreed, forty percent of the blacks between fourteen and twenty-one felt that violence was probably imperative to win their rights.[4]

At the Congress of African People in Atlanta, Georgia, the prevailing mood seemed to be expressed in the words of the general counsel for the group: "It's unfortunate that so many brothers feel so alienated that they have no other recourse but to strike out in this way. And who am I to stop him? That brother knows his own anger better than anyone else."

Two correspondents put the problem in similar terms. William

Raspberry of the *Washington Post:* "Cop-killing is not revolution. Sometimes it's more like suicide. It doesn't take many senseless attacks to get Americans to the point where they will condone virtually any retaliatory move on the part of the police." And Joseph Boyce, a black correspondent, writes: "As a former policeman, I'm placed in a moral dilemma. I am aware that there is a necessity for 'law and order' in its most unadulterated sense. But I am also aware of the need to eliminate what has been a double standard in dealing with blacks and whites. I wish I could say that the sniping will stop. I cannot."

Meanwhile, the issue of "plot" or "contagion" has considerable political mileage. It has been suggested that commissioner Leary, former head of the New York City police department, resigned because Mayor Lindsay refused to probe an alleged plot to kill police. James Buckley, running as the Conservative senatorial candidate in New York asked the governor to name a commission to determine whether the assaults are part of a conspiracy by hate groups. He cited statistics purporting to show that three times as many New York City policemen had been shot in 1970 as the year before. He called the victims "casualties of a war waged by anarchists and barbarians."

POLICE RESPONSE

The reaction from the police in many cities throughout the country has been both in words and deeds. In some places they are being deployed in two-man teams, rather than walking their beats alone. "When you feel scared and they start calling you 'pig' behind your back you like to have someone to back you up. . . . Now, if I'm not looking, I know my partner will be looking."

Some departments are setting up special teams of sharpshooters for use against snipers. Some policemen are agitating to "ride shotgun" in their squad cars. How much such techniques are going to accomplish is problematical. Chief Lacoste concedes: "If someone is really interested in killing a policeman, there is nothing much you can do about it. There are only so many precautions you can take and still be a functioning police department."

Police departments all over the country are stockpiling heavy weapons, even armored cars. Ironically, this is often done with federal funds, provided by the Law Enforcement Assistance Administration. This unit was originally designed to ease urban tensions by providing training in more sympathetic and sophisticated techniques. And in some places, police forces are starting to reconsider the concepts that have guided the organization and functioning of the police for generations, trying to look upon the citizens of the slums, and the members of the blue forces, as human beings, as fellow men rather than antagonists.

The underlying problem has deep and ugly roots. If the self-feeding cycle of hatred and fear between policemen and blacks is not broken, the police will be forced more and more into the role of combat soldier in a hostile territory. "They have to realize," warned Coster, "that the harm they inflict will return against a colleague tomorrow." He added soberly: "The policeman's rapport with the minority community is gone."

Race Friction Among the Police

"We cannot ask the black community to send its lambs to the slaughter, nor will we become Judas goats and lead the young blacks to something that is totally against the very principles of decency and humanity for which we stand."

That sharp answer was made to the Mayor of Pittsburg by the local chapter of the Guardians, a moderate national organization of black policemen.[6] It marked a refusal to help in a drive to recruit more black policemen.

The situation in Pittsburg is one indication of the increasing polarization taking place within police departments. Reports from many many cities across the nation show that relations between white and black policemen vary from open hostility in Pittsburg, to strained in Omaha, to noncommunication in Hartford.

Many of the old-time black police officers have resented what they have felt was discrimination by white colleagues. But the younger blacks on the force refuse to accept the situation with the same equanimity. And the older black policemen are more and more joining younger black recruits in agitating against their grievances.

Some police officers think that things will get worse before they improve. "Frankly, I used to like niggers, but now I hate all of them," a veteran commanding officer of the Omaha Police Department said.[7] He insisted, however, that he did not let his feelings interfere with performance of his duties.

Some policemen are afraid that this friction will eventually lead to an explosion with white and black shooting it out. There have been incidents in Atlanta and Washington in which policemen have drawn guns on each other. The Guardians of Pittsburg assumed their bitter stance on recruitment following a fight between black and white policemen at the annual policeman's picnic.

Some white officers believe that there is a double standard which operates against them and in favor of black policemen. "I had to get my sideburns trimmed while there are Negroes in the precinct wearing Afros, beards and sideburns to their jawbones," claimed a young, white two-year veteran of a Harlem beat. "There is definitely a double standard," he said. "If you are colored, you can get away with murder."

Leaders of the black policemen's groups say that their white colleagues do not understand that black policemen do not share their views about militants, especially Panthers.

There are a few positive signs. Police officials point to young white policemen touring ghetto beats in a number of cities, such as Washington and Atlanta, who seem to get along better with the residents and understand their problems.

TOWARD A NEW POLICY

That no one group has an exclusive monopoly on violence is illustrated by the happenings in Cairo, Illinois. A small, southern oriented town of 8,000, at the conjunction of the Ohio and Mississippi rivers, it was subjected to months of terror. Whites and blacks alike disrupted the silence of the night with gunfire. In a bitter controversy over job discrimination, property owned by both groups has been subjected to intermittent firebombing.

Paradoxically, both races share a common anger against the town's fourteen-man police force—four of whom are black. Ray Burke, a native Virginian, who took over as Cairo's third police chief in two years, finally quit. "White officers don't trust black officers; the black officers don't trust all of the white officers; and the black community doesn't trust any police officer, black or white." Chief Burke explained: "I don't know where I'm going, but I'm looking for a community where people work together."[8]

Former Attorney General Ramsey Clark has stated that the "intermittent warfare" between police officers and blacks in most American cities is largely the result of police prejudice. He cited a report of the President's Crime Commission that found that 72 percent of police interviewed in three major cities were prejudiced against blacks.

Judge George Edwards of the United States Court of Appeals for the Sixth Circuit, has said, "The police are not responsible for solving America's race problem. But if we are to move toward the needed fundamental social changes without something approaching civil war, can anyone doubt the need to re-examine the role of the police in this conflict, and its capacity to meet the challenge?"

Judge Edwards made the following suggestions:[9]

1. To meet ghetto dwellers' demands for equal police protection,

forces should be organized for faster response to ghetto calls; assignments of police should be based on incidence of crime as well as on area.

2. Police departments and ghetto communities should actively seek to set up channels of communication with one another through contact between police and neighborhood leaders, police open-house programs, community workshops, neighborhood advisory councils, meetings with youth groups.

3. In handling demonstrations by potentially hostile groups, police should serve as an agency for serving—not curbing—the public, unless actual violence breaks out. Such organizations should be given the same police assistance in planning peaceful rallies as is provided for other groups.

4. Police officers who are strongly prejudiced against Negroes or sadistic, or who have shown lack of common sense in a crisis, should be assigned to desk jobs or other functions where weaknesses will not come into play.

5. As an alternative to the use of lethal weapons, reliable new methods for temporarily immobilizing offenders should be devised.

6. Police job qualifications and training, including intergroup relations training, should be upgraded, and police pay increased. Forces should be enlarged to reduce excessive case loads. Public opinion should be mobilized to support the demand for the needed additional funds.

7. The federal government should play a major role in the improving and equalizing police services—though financial aid and through a free National Police College.

There can be no simple solutions. But perhaps the best lesson is to be found in the words of Patrick V. Murphy, police commissioner of New York City:[10]

I spent a year and a half walking a beat in an Italian neighborhood. What officers—mostly Irish—said then was very similar to what officers say now about Negroes: "Those Italians never tell you anything. They're not law-abiding like us Irish." Things don't change.

None of those officers knew it was the Irish who were once described as the "criminal element." They didn't know about the Irish riots during the Civil War. You just can't write off a whole neighborhood as the "criminal element" or a "high crime" area. Even in high crime areas, 90 percent of the people are law abiding. They are disproportionate victims of crime. They cry out for good law enforcement.

We can sell ourselves in those communities. When I walked the beat I felt that it was important to say "buono giorno." My wife became a pretty good Italian cook from all the recipes I kept asking for from the ladies on my beat."

XVI.
Toward More Effective Police Work

Evaluating Police Efficiency

ALMOST EVERY DAY, newspapers print letters from irate citizens and armchair quarterbacks who criticize or attack the efficiency of the police. Some demand that law officers resort to tar and feathers or "shoot-first-ask-questions-later" tactics. Some critics are slightly less activist. But very few of those who question police efficiency bother to think through exactly what the police are called upon to do.

Most criticism is directed to the inability of police departments to stem the rising tide of crime. The fears are understandable. The worthy burgher is terrified that he will be garotted in the street, that his daughters will be raped on the way home from school, that his home will be burgled and all his earthly possessions stolen.

As had been indicated, the problem of crime control is in large measure a problem that involves more than the police. Crime prevention and control must involve the entire community. Citizens must be ready to speak up; the public must be prepared to bear the costs of reducing crime. But as well as the financial burden, it must be willing to bear the social and psychic costs of dealing with crime in a meaningful way. Those who have a stake in the existing order must accept a major dislocation of the established structure of our economic, political and social life if our goals are to be approached.

The police are perceived in many roles other than fighting crime. College militants and ghetto residents may see the police as repressive agents of the establishment, rather than as their protectors and guardians of their rights. Some analysts of police function see the policeman as a "troubleshooter"; that is, he is the initial official in the community designated to help the citizen in time of emergency or trouble.

Most of the proposals to upgrade the police are spelled out in terms of higher pay, fancier equipment, better training, additional manpower. Unquestionably, such solutions would be of some help, but, unfortunately, the community does not seem to be too willing to make even the financial expenditures that this would entail. And where public funds have been expended for such purposes, the results have not always convinced the citizenry that the return has been commensurate with the investment.

Perhaps the dissatisfaction comes in part because police performance cannot possibly assuage the frustrations of the public. And perhaps the performance has not been entirely satisfactory because there is confusion concerning what policemen actually do on the job and what they reasonably can be expected to do. If these issues are clarified, it may well be easier to figure out the sort of recruitment, training and equipment that could achieve a more effective police force.

Obviously, the police system is a system for maintenance of law and order. But both the law and the order must be patterned on the underlying philosophy and aspirations of the social system. If the system is to be a democratic one, then the police must support fundamental objectives of a democratic society. The policeman is not a clergyman. He is not a social worker. He is not a physician. He is not a mechanic. He should be able to do his thing, do it as well as he can, with as much help as community support, financial and otherwise, can give him. He should be sensitive to what it means to be a policeman in a political democracy, without being beholden to its political influences.

Cops and Robbers

Every boy has played at "cops and robbers," in which the role of the policeman is always that of catching crooks. To the overwhelming number of adults, this is *the* job of the policeman. And the members of the force undoubtedly see themselves in that role. The top brass of the police departments certainly emphasize that aspect of the work. This stereotype of police work moulds the recruitment, training and equipment policies.

But it has been shown that it is not only the police who are involved in the apprehension of criminals and prevention of crime. What constitutes a crime is usually defined by other agencies—the legislature, for example—and the apprehension of criminals is often impossible due to circumstances beyond the control of the police.

The kinds of acts that are defined as crime reflect in both natur and quantity the society in which they occur. Much crime, especiall crimes of passion and violence, cannot be prevented by better la enforcement since they take place in the family unit or among friend in a flash of anger.

Crime rates may be more affected by the size of the communit the degree to which religion and mores actually support the folkway the visibility or anonymity cloaking the individual, the extent to whic there is a sense of cohesion and interdependence among the citizenr the emphasis on material wealth as status symbols, and other eco nomic and social psychological facts.

The traditional test for the operation of a police department ha been its ability to catch criminals. This is what the professionals an public have always insisted. It is certainly an important part of the job. Everything that interferes with law enforcement is fair game fo police department reforms. Certainly, a police system that is sub jected to criminal control or political tampering must be purged the important job of catching criminals is to be successfully pursued

Certain steps should be taken if the police are to carry out the crime-busting function most effectively. They should be furnishe with the latest scientific know-how and equipment. This may enta the use of sophisticated electronics communication devices and th development of protective weaponry which is not deadly and whic is short lived in its effect on people. The modern techniques of teach ing the new skills in psychology should be of great value in selectin and training better crime fighters, perhaps including the use of aides

Since it is virtually impossible to win the war on crime withou public support and cooperation, measures must be taken to brin about a better relationship between the police and the rest of th community. This involves an enormous task of bridging the gap tha seems to exist between the police on one hand, the minority groups the young people and many ordinary citizens, on the other. It canno be brought about by police action alone, or by citizen action alone but by all working together with recognition of the tremendous stake involved.

As a corollary, to encourage cooperation by citizens in the figh against crime, the courts and the police stations must restructure thei procedures. At the present time, citizens who are involved as wit nesses or complainants often feel as if they were the objects of the criminal law. Many conscientious volunteers find that they lose day after day of their time, as well as their earnings, just because they are fulfilling their duties. They resent the arbitrary and callous manne with which public officials sometimes treat them. The procedures often seem devoid of common sense, or even human feeling.

If the police are to devote more time to fighting crime, there must be some way to relieve them from jobs which should not be the responsibility of their departments. In addition the "troubleshooting" which constitutes over ninety percent of the daily job of the police must be handled in a manner which will permit the force to devote more of its energies to crime fighting. What is often not known, or forgotten, is that at the present time the police catch suspects in only about one quarter of the reported crimes, and less than five percent of these cases result in court convictions.

Among the proposals which have been made, looking to more effective combating of crime, has been the creation of the National Institute of Crime Prevention and Detection. Such facility would serve as a basic research institution which would study all the problems of crime prevention and apprehension. It would help the state and local police agencies by supporting a central research operation at which specialists in many fields could pool their knowledge in the war against crime. It could initiate, encourage, sponsor, and support, research and training programs, starting with inventory and evaluation of the available techniques and equipment for dealing with crime.

A program of workshops throughout the United States would bring in police personnel from all over the country to share specialized skills and general experience. At these round tables, there would be valuable exchange of views with the introduction of new ideas regarding the control of crime and the employment of new techniques and equipment.

There has been enthusiasm among police experts and officials for the Institute for Crime Prevention and Detection. They have suggested a number of subjects for exploration,[1] including "improved police recruitment and training methods; public apathy and antagonism toward the police; the relationship of police work to the courts and probation; more rational use of police forces for surveillance and investigation; ways to anticipate either outbreaks of crime or public disorder; swifter flow of information; computerized storage and dissemination."

Why not flash sketches of suspects or stolen property to police cars within fifty miles, minutes after the perpetration of a crime? How about closed circuited television within places of public assembly or department stores or high crime areas, as is now being tried by the British? More work is needed on devices to identify voices, more accurate and sensitive alarm mechanisms, defensive weapons that can temporarily paralyze. Certainly a good deal of research is required in evaluating the personality traits, the skills, the type of training which can produce the most effective policeman. What is the spectrum of police work? Should some of it be delegated to non-police personnel? Perhaps an auxiliary policeman, indigenous to a particular neighborhood can be effective as a cultural bridge between the police and the community. An institute could focus the attention of professionals from various disciplines to problems of apathy or antagonism. It could deeply study the implications of the "good Samaritan" laws. It could reconsider the implications of compensation for crime victims or rewards for passersby who assist the police. Perhaps it could direct attention to the nature of role playing by the police. Would it not be worthwhile to evaluate methods of crime data gathering and reporting? Without the facts we will never be able to formulate a program which will result in better law enforcement.

Peace Keeping Function

Even taking into account the differences that exist in interpreting details of police work, it is clear that crime-busting does not take up the major portion of a police officer's time. He is generally occupied with other duties, such as getting a sick person to a hospital or finding the mother of a lost child. And when they are not performing these useful acts, policemen are probably busy settling disputes between husband and wife, parent and child, or two lovers. They certainly don't spend a substantial part of their working time pursuing criminals.

There is a real difference between enforcing the law by catching criminals and keeping the peace by rendering service to individual citizens or settling private disputes. In the former function, the policeman is called upon to ferret out those whose conduct does not conform to a statutory standard. The officer must make a preliminary determination as to the conduct of the accused and a preliminary evaluation of whether it falls within the statutory definition. He has to worry about the evidentiary efficacy of what he knows. The policeman, in this context, is not primarily called upon to act as social mediator, he is obligated to simply measure the conduct against the statutory yardstick. Then, if he is satisfied that the law has been broken, he makes an arrest.

When the policeman renders such services as giving directions or mediating a family dispute, no arrest follows. As a matter of fact, in most of such situations, the officer has no basis for making an arrest. He is generally on his own and he cannot look to the structure of the law for guidance. He must look within his own experience, his own skills, his own personality for dealing with the complex problems of human relationships, which he must face in his peace-keeping mission. Historically, this was the prime function of the watchman. The capture of the criminal and the recoupment of loss was the problem of the victim.

The close of the last century saw the basic structure of the modern urban police force and its functional approach take shape. The old police role of "peacekeeper" fell victim to the public anxieties caused by the depression and by the heavy emphasis on "crime" that followed the involvement of the police in the enforcement of prohibition liquor laws.

Responding to widespread criticism of police operations, President Herbert Hoover appointed the Wickersham Commission, the National Commission on Law Observance and Law Enforcement. In its report, the Commission proposed improvements in equipment and personnel. However, proceeding on the assumption that the police are the principal agents for preventing crime, the Commission found the police weakened by the public's failure to support policemen in their crime-fighting function. Unfortunately, this new view overemphasized the importance of police as law enforcers. It also neglected the tremendous importance of the police as peace keepers.

Once the public saw the police in the role of crook catchers (and the police saw themselves playing this role, as well), crime was the cross which the law enforcers had to bear on their broad backs. In spite of more men and more devices, crime did not seem to disappear. As a consequence, to save face and job, perhaps the figures released were adjusted. The "brass" emphasized the importance of a good arrest record or the flamboyant arrest. It was often the *sine qua non* for promotion. The plodding patrolman who spent his twenty years on a beat aiding the community by dozens of quiet acts in maintaining the peace—rather than busting crime—now had to look to heaven for a reward rather than to police headquarters.

Improving Police Work

The President's Commission on Law Enforcement and Administration of Justice, under the directorship of Professor James Vorenberg, submitted its nine-volume report in 1967, without the beat of drums or flare of trumpets. It was matter of fact—it did not blame "politics" for police maladministration; it did not recount juicy scandals. It pointed out that police departments essentially have a different job than the one which is usually attributed to them—not crime fighting requiring force and arms, but rather work that is more social in nature.

It is the thesis of the report that the relationship between crime and policemen is a complex and not easily resolved problem. The ghetto riots, the increasing demand for neighborhood participation in local institutions such as schools and hospitals, the dissension on the campus, certainly require skills other than merely that of a crime fighter.

Crime in the streets is indeed a serious problem and the police must share in the effort to reduce or control it. But the courts, the penal institutions, and every other government agency will have to share this responsibility. And the most important influence in reducing crime must be the home.

The basic dilemma stems from the fact that there must be two departments of police even though they are embraced under a single rubric. Crime fighting needs skilled technicians, clear and unequivocal commands, the capacity to transmit messages and men quickly, certain acquaintance with criminal laws and procedures, insulation from political pressures, investigatory control over the community, and unquestioned honesty.

The peace keeping function calls for a different sort of operation. It emphasizes decentralization and local involvement by the police. It puts a premium on having the patrolman walk the beat, without requiring him to bring in a certain amount of arrests. The policeman must be afforded a wider range of freedom in the way that he deals with his community, must be sensitive to the peculiar folkways, mores and personalities.

Just recently, William V. Shannon[2] in a column dealing with this very subject, wrote:

> This is not to suggest that policemen spend no time catching criminals. But it does indicate that a policeman's relationship with his community is more complicated than first appears. It is a vital relationship which needs all the careful study it can get.

Notes

I. THE POLICEMAN AND PRELIMINARY CRIMINAL PROCEDURES

. *People* v. *Brown*, 32 Misc. 2d 846 (1962).

. *People* v. *Estrialgo*, 233 N.Y.S. 2d 558 (1962).

. *People* v. *Cassone*, 35 Misc. 2d 699 (1962). Some of the complex
diversified problems that the policeman is called upon to solve are de-
bed in the comprehensive study entitled *The Challenge of Crime in a
e Society, A Report of the President's Commission on Law Enforce-
nt and Administration of Justice* (Washington, D.C., 1967). See espe-
ly Chapter 4, "The Police," and Chapter 5, "The Courts."

. Quoted in *Reyes* v. *Rossetti*, 47 Misc. 2d 517 (1965).

. *New York Law Journal*, May 26, 1965, p. 4.

. (1931), p. 16.

. Herbert Wechsler, "A Caveat on Crime Control," 27 J. Crim. L.
Criminology (1937), 629, 634.

. *Miranda* v. *Arizona*, 384 U.S. 436. Law-enforcement officials have
cted quickly in response to the *Miranda* decision. The Police Commis-
er of the City of New York has issued detailed directives to the police,
ructing them as to their obligations with regard to suspects. Similar
on has been taken in most large cities, at least. The Attorney General
Massachusetts has issued an excellent brochure entitled "If You Are
ested," which advises persons detained by the police of their rights.

II. POLICE WORK AND THE CITIZEN

Thomas R. Brooks, "The Finest Could Be Finer," *The New York
es Magazine* (April 3, 1966), p. 28. Considerable support is develop-
for a National Institute of Crime Detection and Prevention. See, e.g.,
euer, "National Institute of Crime Detection and Prevention Needed,"
Student Law Journal (January 1967); *New York Times*, Jan. 25,
7, p. 34; *The Challenge of Crime in a Free Society, supra.*

. *Ibid.*

. *The Challenge of Crime in a Free Society, supra.*

. Dr. Leroy C. Gould, an assistant professor of psychology at Yale
versity, in a report issued on August 20, 1967, has suggested that "be-
se the typical professional doesn't believe he can get a legitimate job,
only solution is to commit more crimes than he normally would."

. September 2, 1967.

III. THE POLICEMAN IN SOCIETY

1. Thomas R. Brooks, "New York's Finest," *Commentary* (Augu 1965), pp. 29-30. John J. Cassese, President of the New York Polic men's Benevolent Association, has expressed the opinion (*New Yo Times,* Sept. 25, 1967) that minority groups in the city were receivir special privileges and often were not being prosecuted for breaking th law. "You can't have two sets of laws or two sets of standards, one fe one group and one for another," he said. "If anyone else disobeyed th law, or was critical, or spat upon policemen, or called them vile name he'd be arrested." It is not an unfair assumption to believe that th opinion finds substantial adherence among other policemen.

2. *Ibid.*

3. *McAuliffe* v. *New Bedford,* 155 Mass. 216 (1892).

4. See survey in New York *World-Telegram and Sun,* Feb. 25, 196

5. Vincent L. Broderick, quoted in *The New Yorker* Magazine (Mar 5, 1966); p. 34.

6. Speech delivered before the Bronx Board of Trade on April 2 1964.

7. New York *Post,* May 3, 1966, p. 57. This columnist's opinion fin some support in an increasing number of news stories. See, e.g., "Whe the Action Is in Boston / Negro Teen-Agers Say 'We're Going to Get th Cops Now,' " *New York Times,* June 6, 1967, p. 36. Perhaps the hippi have the solution. One was quoted by Pete Hamill, New York *Post* colur nist, in his article of July 7, 1967, entitled "The Flower Fuzz":

" 'For a hundred ninety-three years we had trouble with the fuzz,' sa one kid, his hair shoulder-length, bells attached to his wrists and ankl and three walnuts strung around his neck on a piece of thread. 'Alwa' trouble. Always the fuzz bustin' people. Always this hostility, man. Siou City Andy just changed *everything.* That's all.'

"Sioux City Andy decided last year, in a moment of deep religiov vision, that cops were human beings. Repeat: *cops were human being* The reaction was astounding. It was like a man from County Galway di covering that Protestants have souls. Cops were bad. Cops took away po Cops broke heads. Cops had brass knuckles where their hearts should be Sioux City Andy changed it all. It was a kind of landmark religious visior

"While we were talking, one of those giant sun-tanned crinkly-eye L.A. cops parked his car and strolled by, on his way to a cup of coffe He smiled, and you noticed that next to his badge someone had pinned flower."

8. Quoted in the September, 1967, issue of the *Law Enforcement Bu letin,* published by the Federal Bureau of Investigation.
Essays (Charlottesville, Va.: University Press of Virginia, 1965). For a interesting comparison, read Traynor, "The Devils of Due Process i Criminal Detection and Trial," the Cardozo Lecture delivered before th New York Association of the Bar on April 19, 1967, and reprinted in th Record, p. 357.

IV. THE CONSTITUTION IN THE POLICE STATION

1. Yale Kamisar *et al.*, "Criminal Justice in Our Time," *Magna Carta Essays* (Charlottesville, Va.: University Press of Virginia, 1965).

2. 27 J. Crim. L. and Criminology (1937), 629, 637. The conflicting philosophies are often reflected sharply in the comic strips. In "Little Orphan Annie" (New York *Sunday News*, April 16, 1967) we read the following discussion:

"CAPTAIN: Oh, the police have known for weeks who hired that gang to try to kill Pete; the price, the whole plan!

"CITIZEN: Then why aren't they all in jail, captain?

"CAPTAIN: Ah, we're living in a new era! *Now* even admitted violent crime doesn't count! The *legal* question is, *how* the dickens did the cops find out?

"CITIZEN: But that's crazy!

"CAPTAIN: Some of us, in *my* business, think so, but it's the *law*, lady! We also know the men in that group of hired killers! They got back to their home yesterday; but by a recent judicial decision it's illegal for a cop even to ask a suspect his name.

"CITIZEN: Why, that's incredible.

"CAPTAIN: Nope; invasion of the suspect's constitutional right to privacy, said the learned judge!

"CITIZEN: Whose side are the courts on, anyway?

"CAPTAIN: A very good question! I imagine any criminal attorney would be delighted to answer it for a suitable fee!

"CITIZEN: Oh, Peter! Isn't there any protection for *decent* people?"

and then—in a box—what is presumably a comment by the author of the strip, Harold Gray:

"Shucks! Killers! Kidnappers! They're *people*, aren't they? They've got rights! What's the constitution for?"

Contrast the point of view recently expressed by Al Capp, the creator of the comic strip "Li'l Abner." In one panel, a ferocious-looking policeman grabs our hero and Daisy Mae.

"POLICEMAN: YOU'RE UNDER ARREST!!

"COUPLE: ??We haven't mugged nor murdered nobody—

"POLICEMAN: Do you think I'd arrest anybody for anything like THAT, and get MYSELF into trouble? YOU'RE GUILTY OF JAY-WALKING.

"LI'L ABNER: Jay WHAT?"

3. Kamisar, *op. cit.*, p. 118.

REQUIREMENTS OF A VALID ARREST

1. *Detroit Free Press*, Dec. 29, 1960, p. 1. Compare: ". . . The Court feels constrained to say that more than sixteen years of experience . . . compels the conclusion that the disorderly conduct statute is one of the most abused in the entire penal law, by both civilians and the police" *People* v. *Tinston*, 163 N.Y.S. 2d 554 [1957]). From time to time, the

daily newspapers quote various law-enforcement officers, calling for clean-up campaign in certain neighborhoods. Sanford Garelik, Chief I spector of the New York City Police Department, in one such stateme (*New York Times,* March 16, 1966), referred to these areas of the ci as "targets for some of the more disreputable elements of our socie [which] require our immediate and urgent attention." The drive would I directed at "prostitution, derelicts, degenerates, alcoholics"; this would I followed by "increased police activity."

2. *Report and Recommendations of the Commissioner's Committ on Police Arrests for Investigation* (Washington, D.C., 1962), p. 34.

A case with important implications is *Morales v. New York,* 38 L.V 4023. There, the New York Court of Appeals had approved in princip "an investigatory arrest," an "arrest without probable cause." The S preme Court was not convinced that "probable cause" was absent. It ser the case back for factual findings.

3. Quoted in *United States* v. *Bonanno,* 180 F. Supp. 71, 78.

4. *Lester* v. *Albers Super Markets, Inc.,* 94 Ohio App. 313.

VI. USE OF FORCE BY A POLICEMAN OR A CITIZEN

1. See, *e.g., State* v. *Paschall,* 197 Wash. 582 (1939).

2. It is unfortunate, but community attitudes toward the use of forc by the police are becoming more and more polarized. In New York, as September 1, 1967, the Penal Code has been very substantially revise Article 35 of this law, dealing with the lawful use of force, imposes su stantial restrictions on the right of a police officer to use deadly physic force in arrest situations. It is feared, on one hand, that this will serious impede the policeman from protecting himself and from apprehendin criminals. On the other hand, it is urged that such restraints are necessar to protect the individual from abusive treatment at the hands of th police. Criticism of the way in which the police use force is not uncom mon. See, e.g., "Police Brutality Charged on Coast," *New York Time.* Aug. 2, 1967, p. 15; "Negroes in Nyack Assail Arrests / Call Polic 'Trigger-Happy' / Whites Defend Action," *New York Times,* Oct. 6, 196 p. 43; "College Virtually Closed as 80% of Students Strike over Actio by Police," *New York Times,* Oct. 21, 1967, p. 1.

More and larger recoveries are being awarded for suits based upo police action. See, e.g., New York *Post,* June 16, 1967, p. 18: "A Brook lyn longshoreman who claimed that he had been beaten by two polic officers 'like an animal in a cage' won a $145,000 suit against the cit yesterday—the largest award made in a police brutality case."

VII. SEARCH AND SEIZURE

1. The house-to-house search for allegedly stolen weapons conducte in a Negro section of Plainfield, New Jersey, which was carried out b state troopers and National Guardsmen in July of 1967, lasted for only few hours. The legal issues relating to the validity of the searches, how ever, will go on being debated for many years. The critical questio appears to be whether or not Governor Richard J. Hughes' declaration o a state of emergency in the city torn by riots was a valid legal reason fo

ermitting searches without proper warrants.

2. In June of 1967, the Supreme Court of the United States delivered six decisions relating to the constitutionality of electronic surveillance. In *Berger* v. *New York*, 18 L. Ed. 2d 1040, the Court seems to have decided that it is technically possible to use electronic devices legally. It is questionable, however, whether regulations that comply with the direction of the Court can ever work in practice.

On December 18, 1967, in *Katz* v. *United States*, the Supreme Court authorized electronic eavesdropping, provided the police obtain a warrant in advance.

3. In June of 1967, the majority of the Supreme Court of the United States held that administrative inspectors must obtain search warrants when householders do not wish to give them admittance to their homes for the purpose of making inspections. In one case, Ronald Camara, the owner of a bookstore, had admittedly violated the city building code by residing in the rear of his store. His conviction—for refusing to allow a building inspector to see the premises without a warrant—was reversed. The Court also set aside a conviction for a refusal to permit a fire inspector to check a locked warehouse for possible violations. However, the Court also made it easier to obtain a warrant. Inspectors need not show "probable cause," specifying that a particular violation has occurred, before they make a search. Instead, warrants for "area inspections" may be issued simply because an area is due for an inspection. In addition, Justice White pointed out that searches without warrants are still permitted in emergencies, such as for control of fire or disease.

Although U.S. Treasury Agents are authorized to make a warrantless entry and inspection of a liquor licensee's premises, they cannot do so forcibly, even though the licensee's refusal to allow a warrantless entry is a criminal offense. *Colonnade Catering Corp.* v. *U.S.*, 38 L.W. 4167.

4. The New York and Ohio "stop and frisk" laws are under review by the United States Supreme Court. In both these states, a citizen may be stopped and searched by a policeman on the mere suspicion that he may be doing something unlawful. Evidence turned up by this search can be used against him in court. *New York* v. *Taggart*, decided by the New York Court of Appeals on July 7, 1967, illustrates this problem.

The police were told in an anonymous telephone call that an eighteen-year-old white youth, who had blue eyes and blond hair and was wearing white chino-type pants, was standing at a specified corner and had a loaded thirty-two-caliber revolver in his left-hand jacket pocket. When a detective arrived at the location, he saw a young man, who matched the description perfectly, standing in the middle of a group of children. He took the youth by the arm, put him against a wall, and took a revolver out of his left-hand jacket pocket. The search was held valid under the state "stop and frisk" law, and the introduction of the revolver at the trial was held not to have violated the defendant's constitutional rights.

In *Terry* v. *Ohio*, 36 L.W. 4578, the Court upheld the right of the police, with less than probable cause for arrest, to pat down suspicious individuals they have reason to believe are dangerous. It is limited to a carefully made search of the outer clothing of such persons in the attempt to discover weapons that might be used to assault the policeman. It is permissible only "where a police officer observes unusual conduct which

leads him reasonably to conclude in the light of his experience th
criminal activity may be afoot and that the persons with whom he
dealing may be armed and presently dangerous; where in the course
investigating this behavior he identifies himself as a policeman and mak
reasonable inquiries, and where nothing in the initial stages of the e
counter serves to dispel his reasonable fear for his own or others' safety
5. 87 S. Ct. 1642 (1967).

The search of a defendant's house for narcotics, without a warrar
incident to his arrest on the front steps of his house was held a violati
of the Fourth Amendment by a majority of the Court held in *Vale
Louisiana*, 38 L.W. 4544. And in *U.S. v. Van Leeuwen*, 38 L.W. 422
postal officials, who detained a suspicious looking package for 29 hou
while waiting to get a search warrant, did not violate the Fourth Amen
ment by their delay.

6. Some recent cases have reflected a stiffening of the courts' previous
rather liberal attitude toward the searching of automobiles.

On August 24, 1961, in Dallas, a gunman with a handkerchief coverin
the lower part of his face held up the Tower Motel coffee shop. A fe
minutes later, a policeman stopped an automobile for having a noisy mu
fler. Something about the automobile and the two men in it aroused th
officer's suspicions; he proceeded to search the vehicle and found a bag
money, a handkerchief, and a pistol.

Witnesses subsequently identified one of the two, Daniel Grundstron
as the man who had robbed the coffee shop. A district court jury sent hi
to the penitentiary for twenty-five years.

On August 24, 1966, five years later, United States District Judge W
M. Taylor, Jr., ruled that the search had been illegal and that Grundstror
must be released. The district attorney has appealed this ruling; pendin
the outcome of the appeal, therefore, Grundstrom is still in prison. Bu
critics of recent high court decisions have described this case as one mor
in a long list of cases in which the criminal is given more of a break tha
his victim.

The changing viewpoint of the courts with regard to such searches wa
clearly indicated in another 1967 case. The California Highway Patro
suspended vehicle safety inspections in Santa Barbara County after Supe
rior Court Judge Preston Butcher, in considering this case, called int
question that section of the California Vehicle Code relating to inspections

On August 19, the Highway Patrol had stopped an automobile nea
Santa Barbara for a routine safety check. In the car were a young ma
and his girl, both nineteen years old. One of the officers noticed the ma
stuffing something under the seat of the car; it proved to be a package o
marijuana. The couple was arrested and charged with possession of mari
juana. At the trial, however, Judge Butcher dismissed those charges be
cause he questioned the procedures by which the marijuana was found

In *Chambers v. Maroney*, 386 L.W. 4547, the Court expressly statec
that policemen who have "probable cause" to search a car at the time
and place of arrest do not violate the Fourth Amendment by carrying on
a warrantless search at another time and place several hours after the
arrest. However the Court reaffirmed *Chimel v. California*, 395 U.S. 694
in which the Court explicitly recognized a difference between search of a
building and a search of an easily moved vehicle.

Johnson v. *United States*, 333 U.S. 10 (1948).
Mapp v. *Ohio*, 368 U.S. 871 (1961).

VIII. ILLEGAL DETENTION AND REMEDIES

State v. *Mulvaney*, 21 N.J. Super. 457, 560 (1952).
Cincencia v. *La Gay*, 357 U.S. 504 (1958).
Secret Detention by the Chicago Police (Glencoe, Ill.: The Free
ss, 1959), p. 13.
Carafas v. *La Vallee*, 36 L.W. 4409.
Walker v. *Wainwright*, 36 L.W. 3357.

IX. RELEASE BEFORE TRIAL—THE RIGHT TO BAIL

. It has been pointed out, interestingly enough, that the nations that
this explanation for denying bail express it in terms of apprehension
the accused commit *another* crime while released. Of course, this
mes that the accused is guilty of the crime for which he has not as
been tried.
. Quoted in Wizner, "Bail and Civil Rights," *Law in Transition* Q.
(1965), p. 116.
. *Stack* v. *Boyle*, 242 U.S. 1 (1951).
. Bernard Botein, "Bail Reform Vital for Equal Justice," *Trial* (Oct./
v. 1965), p. 18.
. *Butler* v. *Crumlish*, 229 F. Supp. 565, 568 (1964).
. *White* v. *United States*, 330 F. 2d 811 (1964), p. 814.
. *United States* v. *Hinton*, 283 F. Supp. 230, 231 (1965).
. *Bandy* v. *United States*, 81 Supreme Court 197 (1960).
. Botein, *loc. cit.*
. A part-time maid was locked up in a New York City jail on a
rge of possession of narcotics. She could not secure her freedom be-
se she was unable to furnish the twenty-five dollars bail required to be
ted. She had been confined for twenty days when the charge was
lly proved to be without foundation; the police laboratory test showed
t the "narcotics," which had been so described by a neighbor, were
hing more than vitamin pills. By that time, the wretched woman had
her job and been dispossessed from her apartment.
There would be less cause for concern if this unfortunate incident were
isolated aberration. However, as was pointed out in a report of the
ited States Senate in 1965, "Thousands of citizens are confined each
r, not because they are guilty of the commission of a crime, but be-
se they cannot afford to post bail."

X. CONFESSIONS—THE METHOD OF INTERROGATION

. *New York Times*, Dec. 14, 1965, p. 28; see also *New York Times*,
e 14, 1966, pp. 1, 25.
. *New York Times*, Nov. 20, 1965, p. 1; see also *New York Law
rnal* series written by Judge Sobel, "The Exclusionary Rules in the
w of Confessions," Nov. 15, 1965, p. 1, et. seq.
. *Watts* v. *Indiana*, 338 U.S. 49 (1949).

4. *Fikes* v. *Alabama*, 352 U.S. 1991 (1957).

5. *Blackburn* v. *Alabama*, 361 U.S. 199, 206 (1960).

6. Jerome and Barbara Frank, *Not Guilty* (New York: Doubleday, 1957), pp. 180-181.

7. *Townsend* v. *Sain*, 372 U.S. 293, 307-308 (1963).

8. 36 L.W. 447.

9. *Delli Paolli* v. *U.S.*, 352 U.S. 232.

10. *Mathis* v. *U.S.*, 36 L.W. 4379.

11. *Harrison* v. *U.S.*, 36 L.W. 4549.

XI.   THE RIGHT TO COUNSEL

1. *New York Times*, Feb. 25 1966, p. 1.

2. Tentative Draft No. 1, March 1, 1966.

3. *New York Times*, March 2, 1966.

4. 372 U.S. 335 (1963).

5. *Malloy* v. *Hogan*, 378 U.S. 1 (1964).

6. 378 U.S. 478 (1964).

7. The Supreme Court, on June 13, 1966, rendered its decision Miranda v. *Arizona*, 384 U.S. 436, and in three other appeals, all brought by prisoners who had confessed after having been interrogated by the police. On June 20, 1966, it disposed of two additional appeals involving related questions.

8. *New York Times*, June 14, 1966, p. 25.

9. 372 U.S. 335 (1963).

10. *New York Times*, June 20, 1966, p. 15.

11. *Ibid.*

12. *New York Times*, Feb. 28, 1966, p. 18.

13. *New York Times*, March 13, 1966, p. 12-E.

14. *Ibid.*

15. *New York Times*, Dec. 23, 1965, p. 33.

16. *New York Times*, March 13, 1966, p. 12-E.

XII.   REVIEW OF COMPLAINTS AGAINST THE POLICE

1. *New York Times*, July 12, 1966, p. 33.

2. *Ibid.*, p. 42.

3. *New York Times*, March 24, 1966, p. 35.

4. *New York Times*, April 9, 1966, p. 34.

5. New York *World-Telegram and Sun*, Feb. 16, 1966, pp. 1, 4.

XIII.   LAW ENFORCEMENT IN THE GREAT SOCIETY

1. *The Public Interest*, Fall 1966.

2. *Miranda* v. *Arizona*, 384 U.S. 436 (1966).

3. 87 S. Ct. 1642 (1967).

4. 18 L. Ed. 2d 1040 (1967).

5. 87 S. Ct. 1428 (1967).

XIV.   POLICE ON THE CAMPUS

1. *New York Post*, Sept. 28, 1970, p. 4.

2. *Ibid.*

3. June 24, 1968.

4. 379 U.S. 536 (1965).

5. "Rights to Demonstrate," *Columbia Journal of Law & Social Problems*, Oct. 24, 1966.

6. *Feiner v. New York*, 340 U.S. 315 (1951).

7. 372 U.S. 229 (1963).

8. 279 U.S. 536 (1965).

9. *New York Times*, Jan. 21, 1968, p. 1.

10. *United States v. O'Brien*, No. 232, 36 U.S. *Law Week*, 4469, decided May 27, 1968.

XV.   POLICE IN THE GHETTO

1. *New York Times*, Sept. 4, 1970, pp. 1, 67.

2. *New York Times*, Sept. 8, 1970, pp. 1, 32.

3. *New York Times*, Oct. 2, 1970, pp. 1, 18.

4. *Time*, Sept. 14, 1970, p. 13.

5. *New York Times*, Sept. 13, 1970, p. 86.

6. *Time*, Oct. 5, 1970, p. 10.

7. *New York Times*, Sept. 12, 1970, p. 33.

8. *Time*, Oct. 5, 1970, p. 10.

9. *New York Law Journal*, July 9, 1970, p. 1.

10. *New York Times*, Sept. 12, 1970, p. 33.

XVI.   TOWARD MORE EFFECTIVE POLICE WORK

1. Scheuer, James H., "National Institute of Crime Detection and Prevention Needed," *The Student Law Journal*, January, 1967.

2. *New York Times*, Sept. 6, 1970, p. 10.

Index

More Arco Books You'll Want to Own

CIVIL RIGHTS AND RESPONSIBILITIES UNDER THE CONSTITUTION
Sidney H. Asch

A comprehensive analysis of the most disturbing questions facing Americans today—narcotics, use of firearms, censorship, demonstrations, draft dodging. **"Primarily designed for the layman, the book is legally accurate and highly readable ... highly recommended."—Library Journal** $4.95

CRIME, THE LAW, AND YOU
Robert A. Farmer

An explanation of the laws in all fifty states affecting murder, manslaughter, rape, assault and battery. Includes the legal rights of a citizen accused of a crime. $4.95

DIVORCE AND ANNULMENT
Michael F. Mayer

A layman's guide to the laws governing termination of marriage in all fifty states—adultery, desertion, mental cruelty, incompatibility and others. Also covered are separation agreements, child support, alimony. **"Clear, comprehensive, well-organized."**
—Family Life Clothbound, $4.95
Paperbound, $1.45

THE HOMOSEXUAL AND THE LAW
Roger S. Mitchell

A look at the special legal problems facing the homosexual in our society—police harassment, discrimination in employment, more. $4.95

HOW TO ADOPT A CHILD
Robert A. Farmer

A complete guide for the couple eager to adopt a child yet confused by the multiplicity of laws, regulations and requirements affecting adoption procedures. Covered here are selection of the child, who may adopt, religion and race requirements, public and private agencies, federal and state regulations. $4.95

HOW TO AVOID PROBLEMS WITH YOUR WILL
Robert A. Farmer

A simple explanation in layman's language of all the intricacies connected with the writing and execution of a will—how to make a will, rights of spouse and children, different types of provisions, tax problems, how a will can be revoked, more. $4.95

HOW TO COLLECT ON PERSONAL INJURIES
Robert A. Farmer

Everything you should know about the law of liability in regard to the automobile, the home, the consumer, the employee, the government. Includes vital information on proof of causation in an automobile accident, homeowner's liability for negligence and workmen's compensation. $4.95

THE RIGHTS OF THE MENTALLY ILL
Robert A. Farmer

A concise summary of the legal consequences of mental illness and mental retardation covering insanity and the legal process, statutory definitions, psychiatrists and the law, the need for legal protection, incompetency proceedings, hospitalization, commitment and release, domestic and family effects, legal effects on property, civil rights. $4.95

THE TEACHER AND THE LAW
Laurence Kallen

A guide to the laws governing pupil control and liability in all of the 50 states—the teacher's duties on the school grounds, during recess, in the classroom and the hallways are covered as are his rights regarding enforcement of rules, searching a desk, using corporal punishment and self-defense. $4.95

THE TRUTH ABOUT INHERITANCE
Robert A. Farmer

Vital facts about inheritance of concern to everyone—how property can be passed to heirs, the duties of trusts and trustees, life insurance, wrongful death actions, taxation on inherited property, how to provide a tax-free inheritance for your family. $4.95

WHAT YOU SHOULD KNOW ABOUT CONTRACTS
Robert A. Farmer

A complete guide to contract law for the layman which outlines the requirements for a valid contract—proper parties, the offer, its acceptance, considerations, form and certainty—explains how to interpret a contract, discusses remedies for dissolution and breach of contract and clarifies the Uniform Commercial Code.
     $4.95

WHAT YOU SHOULD KNOW ABOUT LIBEL AND SLANDER
Michael F. Mayer

Vivid reconstructions of famous and infamous cases of defamation. What is the distinction between libel and slander? Does the law of libel clash with the right of free speech? What protection does a public official have against being defamed? Can a man be libelled by being put on a blacklist? $4.95
